Mrs. Patricia Ann Bonacari
2 Allingworth Ave.
Tenafly, New Jersey 07670

# The Pleasures of Preserving and Pickling

# The Pleasures of
# Preserving and Pickling

## Jeanne Lesem

ILLUSTRATIONS BY JULIE MAAS

Alfred A. Knopf  New York

1975

*This Is a Borzoi Book*
*Published by Alfred A. Knopf, Inc.*

Grateful acknowledgment is made to the following for permission to reprint previously published recipes:

Alfred A. Knopf, Inc. and James A. Beard: "Olive Oil Pickles" from *Beard on Food*. Copyright © 1974 by James A. Beard.

Jewell Fenzi and Helen Dovale: "Ponche Crema" from *This is the Way We Cook!* (asina nos ta cushina). Copyright © 1971 by Jewell Fenzi and Helen Dovale.

Atheneum Publishers: "Sweet-Sour Plum Relish," "Saure Pflumli," from *The Swiss Cookbook* by Nika Standen Hazelton. Copyright © 1967 by Nika Standen Hazelton.

101 Productions: "Peach Jam" from *The Calculating Cook* by Jeanne Jones. Copyright © 1971 by Jeanne Jones.

**Library of Congress Cataloging in Publication Data**
Lesem, Jeanne.
The pleasures of preserving and pickling.
Includes index.
1. Canning and preserving.   I. Title.
TX601.L38      641.4      74–21323
ISBN 0–394–48922–5

Published June 20, 1975
Second Printing, August 1975

This book is dedicated to
my mother, Jeanette Schwartz, who taught me to cook,
and to Gay Pauley Sehon, who first encouraged me
to write about cooking.

# Contents

# Introduction

Growing up in Arkansas during the Depression, I became keenly aware of the value of preserves and pickles. No matter how tight our budget, Mother always managed to put up garlicky dill pickles (from cucumbers no larger than a finger) and preserves from homegrown grapes, berries, and peaches. She made watermelon pickles and pickled peaches to eat with fried chicken and our Thanksgiving goose; piccalilli and chow-chow to go with hamburgers, hot dogs, and cold cuts. Every meal, no matter how plain, tasted better when there was something sweet or spicy, sharp or tangy, to go with it. Even breakfast was worth getting up for when there was Mother's Concord grape preserve for my morning toast. In fact, I became so spoiled by these treats that I found it hard to do without them when I moved to the city and had only my memories of their delicious flavors. I also missed the fun of preserving and the sharp, spicy smells that wafted through the house at pickling time.

Today more than ever I find that people share this nostalgia — we long for the old traditions, cherish handed-down recipes, and find great satisfaction in putting up preserves and pickles the way our grandmothers did — without strange-sounding chemical additives and ersatz flavors. The act of preserving has become doubly rewarding, for not only are we following old traditions, but we are also saving good things at the peak of their flavor and quality. And this gives a great sense of accomplishment, particularly at a time when we are so conscious of waste and skyrocketing prices.

Still, there are many who would like to make preserves and pickles at home but who hesitate to try, especially if they live in cities or have only a small kitchen and limited storage space. It is with them in mind that I have written this book, containing recipes I have made time and again in my own 8- by 9-foot kitchen.

Ideally, the fruits and vegetables you preserve should be put up the day they are picked. This is easy if you have a garden or live near a farm or a farmers' market. But city folk can create perfectly delicious things with produce bought at sidewalk stands and supermarkets. The secret here lies in recognizing quality, freshness, and ripeness; and in my first chapter I tell you how to do just that.

You also should choose locally grown produce in preference to the kind that has been shipped for miles and days. Tropical and semi-tropical fruits such as bananas, oranges, lemons, limes, grapefruit, and pineapple are obvious exceptions. Rare items like quinces are worth seeking out, and they are likely to be expensive. In some seasons I have paid almost a dollar each for them, but their flavor and fragrance are so irresistible that to me they are worth preserving. For the most part, though, ingredients for homemade preserves and pickles are not costly. One of my favorite relishes is my version of an imported French chutney that costs about four dollars for a jar of less than eight ounces. My adaptation ended up costing about fifty cents — and I think it tastes better, too. You will also find my homemade wine jellies far less expensive than any you can buy.

Don't be deterred by the thought of buying a lot of expensive and hard-to-store utensils. Most of the things you need are probably in your kitchen already. Your preserving kettles can be the saucepans you use daily for cooking many other things; the sterilizer, a large covered pot of the sort used for boiling spaghetti and corn on the cob. You can order an old-fashioned jar lifter by mail or find one at a hardware store or housewares department, but inexpensive squeeze tongs sold at stores throughout the United States work just as safely and well for removing jars from the sterilizer.

Preserving on a small scale is not awesomely time-consuming, and it is so easy. Moreover, you can put aside most homemade preserves and pickles at one stage or another to finish at your convenience. In other words, you need not stand for hours over a hot stove during a heat wave or if you're just plain tired.

While most pickles and preserves are quick to make, many are slow to mature. Like red wines that improve with bottle age, pickles and relishes and even a few preserves and marmalades benefit from storage periods ranging from a few weeks to a month or more. On the other hand, most jams, jellies, preserves, and marmalades are like white wines—best consumed before age destroys their color and flavor. If you have a problem with storage in a small apartment, you can always find room on the floor of a closet—preferably away from the heat of the kitchen—to hold a few small jars for a while. In individual recipes I have suggested minimum storage times, and sometimes maximum storage. Tempting as it may be to open jars at once, do be patient; you will find everything tastes better when it has had a chance to mellow.

Gathering these recipes has been a lifelong pleasure. For years I have collected them the way many people collect antiques, searching always for the best in quality and appearance. The one hundred or so in this book are my favorites and I hope they will become yours. Some are old-fashioned recipes reduced to manageable proportions for small kitchens and small households. Others are adaptations of normally expensive products. Still others are my own inventions. A few are West Indian recipes I discovered while traveling. A substantial number are family favorites generously shared by relatives, friends, and friends of friends. While I have been specific in most recipes, I hope you will learn to improvise, to rely on your own taste.

I have not tried to trace every recipe to its primary source, but whenever possible I have identified individual contributors. My thanks go to them and to my many volunteer tasters who also contributed suggestions for using preserves and pickles in new and sometimes unconventional ways.

I am particularly grateful to Maidie Alexander Scannell and Demetria Taylor, for putting me up as well as putting up with me during heat waves and harvest seasons; Eleanor Lowenstein of the Corner Book Shop, for locating old cookbooks; and Evelyn Funt, Hannah Gornick, and Marjorie Griffiths, for helping with the tedious job of proofreading.

*Jeanne Lesem*
New York, New York
February, 1975

# Observations

# Shopping Tips

Many fruits and vegetables used for preserving and pickling can be bought the year round, especially at urban and suburban supermarkets and produce stands. But you're more apt to get the best quality and flavor and the lowest prices if you shop at the peak of your local or regional harvest season or, at least, the peak season for nationally distributed, mass-produced crops.

The list that follows indicates peak season nationally for most of the fruits and vegetables called for in this book. With the exception of chestnuts, quinces, shallots, and green tomatoes, the information about crops comes from the United Fresh Fruit and Vegetable Association.

I have suggested September through October as the peak season for green tomatoes because that is the end of the growing season in most areas of the United States, and the fruit must be picked, ripe or not, before first frost. Green tomatoes usually are plentiful then at farm stands and in city markets; in the retail stores they may not always be on display, but I've found clerks are happy to bring out the green fruit from the storeroom where it is ripening.

Apples — October – March
Bananas — All Year
Beets — July
Blueberries — June – August
Cabbage — All Year
Carrots — January – April
Cauliflower — September – November
Cherries — June – July
Chestnuts — September 15 – December
Corn — June – August
Cranberries — November
Cucumbers — May – July
Grapefruit — November – April
Grapes, Concord — September – October

Honeydew melon—August—September
Lemons—May—August
Limes—June—July
Nectarines—July—August
Onions—All Year
Oranges—November—March
Peaches—June—August
Pears—August—October
Pears (forelle)—November
Pears (seckel)—Late August—November
Peppers, bell or sweet—June—September
Peppers, hot or chili—June—September
Pineapple—March—May
Plums—June—September
Quinces—Late October—November
Raspberries—June—July
Rhubarb—April—May
Shallots—November—April
Strawberries—April—June
Tangerines—November—January
Tomatoes, green—September—October
Tomatoes, ripe—May—August
Watermelon—June—July

# Ripeness and Quality

**Apples**—Skin color varies according to variety. Avoid bruised and blemished fruit. Summer varieties tend to be more tart and tender than those harvested in the fall and winter. No single variety is available nationally. Depending on where you live, you should be able to find one or more of the following in markets between July and September: Crimson Beauty, Early McIntosh, Julyred, Lodi, Melba, Puritan, Summer Champion, Summer Rambo, Tydeman's Red, and Williams Red.

**Bananas**—For preserving and pickling, firm, slightly underripe fruit is best. It will have yellow peel with no dark spots, and sometimes be tinged with green at stem end.

**Beets**—Firm, round, with slender main root, deep red color and smooth surface. Avoid oval-shaped beets with scaly top surface, indicating toughness.

**Blueberries**—Deep blue with whitish bloom, nature's waxy protective coating. Unripe berries are reddish blue.

**Cabbage**—Firm, hard heads, heavy for their size, good pale to deep green or red color, depending on variety, and free from blemishes.

**Carrots**—Well formed, smooth, firm, brightly colored, free from splits or wilting.

**Cauliflower**—Compact, solid, white to creamy white curds, bright green jacket leaves. Avoid speckled or discolored heads.

**Cherries**—Dark sweet ones, deep red, almost black; unripe ones are bright red. Sour cherries are bright red, soft and juicy when ripe.

**Chestnuts**—Glossy brown unsplit shells. Breaks in the shell or sprouting may indicate mold or other spoilage. Store in refrigerator or freezer.

**Corn**—Fresh-looking husks with bright color, silk ends free from injury or decay, and kernels that are plump but not too mature.

**Cranberries**—Deep burgundy red color and unblemished. Unripe ones are bright red.

**Cucumbers**—Firm, good green to whitish green color, smallish diameter. Avoid yellowish ones and those with shriveled ends, indicating bitterness and toughness.

**Grapefruit**—Look for fruit heavy for its size; this indicates juiciness. A large fruit that seems light for its size is liable to be dry and have little flavor. Blemishes on the peel, such as russet spots and green streaks, are freaks of nature and do not affect the flavor, quality, or juice content.

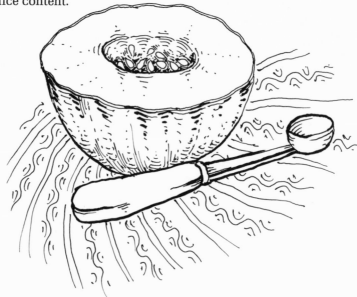

**Grapes, Concord** — Deep purple. Mature, unripe ones are reddish.

**Honeydew melon** — Rind color, white to creamy white; blossom end springy to soft, with a fruity, spicy aroma when cut. Fully mature but unripe melons (the best type for preserving and pickling) have white rinds with only traces of green; blossom ends are hard to springy, and fruit lacks aroma.

**Lemons** — For a recipe that calls for juice and grated peel, choose smooth-skinned fruit that gives easily to hand pressure, indicating thin peel and much juice. But for marmalades and recipes using sliced, whole fruit, select rough-skinned ones that are quite firm, indicating thick peel and less juice.

**Limes** — Bright green color, with no soft, yellowish spots, indicating overripeness.

**Mint** — Bright green leaves with no brown spots or other indications of insect damage.

**Nectarines** — Rich reddish cheeks on orange-yellow ground or, for some varieties, greenish ground color. A slight softening can be felt with gentle hand pressure along the seam when fruit is ripe.

**Onions** — Brittle, papery skin and no soft or moldy spots. Sprouting or hollow, woody centers indicate spoilage.

**Oranges** — Navel and temple, with their thick, easily removable peels, are best for marmalades and conserves for which pectin content is a primary consideration. The white pith just beneath the colored peel contains a lot of pectin. Thin-skinned varieties such as Valencias, Hamlins, and pineapples tend to yield more juice. The pineapple variety's high seed content is an advantage in a recipe calling primarily for juice. You can extract natural pectin by soaking the seeds in a few spoonfuls of water, then boiling them separately or with the other ingredients. Juicy oranges are heavy for their size. Russet spots do not affect the flavor or juice content, nor do green spots on the skin. This regreening is caused by weather changes and has no effect on the sweetness or acidity of the fruit.

**Peaches**—Ground color, or background, is yellowish to creamy, and texture is firm or fairly firm. A red color, called blush, also indicates ripeness, but the blush alone is not a reliable test. Look carefully for bruise marks which indicate spoilage.

**Pears**—Color depends on variety. Bartletts and comice are pale golden yellow when ripe; Anjous are pale green, sometimes tinged with yellow. Ripe seckel pears are dull brownish yellow blushed with dull red. Ripe forelle pears are highly colored with bright red blush and red freckles on golden yellow ground. Ripen pears in closed paper (not plastic) bag at room temperature out of direct sunlight.

**Peppers, sweet and hot**—Fully ripe ones range from scarlet to deep red. Partly ripe ones, streaked with pink, ripen easily within a few days if enclosed in a paper bag on a counter out of direct sunlight. The bag traps gas given off naturally by the vegetable to make it ripen.

**Pineapple**—Forget the old saw about pulling a leaf from the prickly crown. That's more a test of your strength than it is the fruit's ripeness. A fully ripe pineapple has a fresh-looking deep green crown and a pronounced aroma at room temperature. But most markets keep pineapples so well chilled the aroma test is rarely possible. Shell, or skin, color does not indicate ripeness. A ripe fruit will give slightly to finger pressure. And in the end, the best way to shop for this fruit is to look for the signs of spoilage. Avoid any pineapples that have an old, dry, brownish crown, an unpleasant odor, watery, dry eyes, and traces of mold which is liable to start first at the stem end. The largest fruit are the best buys. A 2- to 3-pound pineapple contains less than 30 percent edible flesh, but half of a 5-pound one has more flesh than a whole pineapple weighing 3 to 3½ pounds.

**Plums, Italian or prune variety**—Deep, purplish blue with whitish bloom, nature's protective coating; slight give when pressed with fingers. Mature but unripe plums are reddish blue.

**Plums, Santa Rosa variety**—Deep pink blush on pale, yellowish ground color; texture, fairly firm to slightly soft. Mature but unripe fruit will be firm and lighter in color. Immature plums will be relatively hard, with poor color and, sometimes, signs of shriveling.

**Quinces**—Pale golden yellow but hard when ripe, and always knobby in shape. The gray fuzz that appears naturally on the skins should be rubbed off with a dry towel, and some markets do this before putting the fruits on display. Ripe quinces also have a delightfully spicy scent. Avoid green ones with no traces of yellow—they are so immature that they are liable to shrivel before they ripen.

**Raspberries, red**—Deep, pinkish red, free from blemishes and mold.

**Rhubarb**—For preserving, the palest pink varieties are best, even pale pink tinged with green. Avoid stalks that are too thin or too thick, indicating stringiness and toughness. Avoid wilted stalks. Deep red varieties produce a less appetizing color in jam than lighter-colored ones.

**Shallots**—Brown, papery outer skin, no signs of softness, sprouting or mold.

**Strawberries**—Deep, bright red, and fresh looking, with bright green caps. The best for preserving are mature but not fully ripe—they should be much lighter in color than fully ripe berries.

**Tangerines**—Bright orange skin, relatively free from blemishes and fruit heavy for its size.

**Tomatoes, mature green**—Glossy skin that cannot be torn by scraping with fingernail or knife, seeds that are pushed aside rather than cut when the tomatoes are sliced, and well-formed jellylike substance in the seed chambers. Color ranges from medium to pale green, sometimes lightly streaked with pink.

**Tomatoes, ripe**—Color depends on varieties; they range from golden yellow to deep orange-red. The best are firm, plump, fairly well shaped, smooth, and free from blemishes. Scars at the blossom end do not affect flavor, but tomatoes with growth cracks should not be used for preserving and pickling because they spoil faster than unblemished ones.

**Watermelon**—The only true test for ripeness is cutting and tasting. As the quantity needed for the watermelon pickle recipe in this book is small, your best buy is a quarter or half melon with characteristic deep-pink flesh and the thickest skin you can find.

## *Peeling Produce*

Ripe tomatoes, ripe peaches, and most plums usually peel easily if they are immersed in boiling water for a few seconds. If you have a wire salad basket with a bucket handle, fill it with a single layer of fruit and dip it first into a pan of boiling water and then into a large bowl

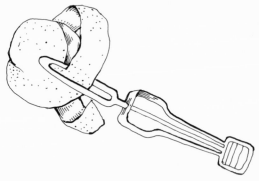

of cold tap water until the fruit can be handled easily. The skins should lift off without difficulty. If not, dip the fruit into the boiling water a few seconds longer. Unripe tomatoes, peaches, plums, apples and pears require a swivel-blade peeler or a small sharp knife. Some ripe nectarines can be peeled like ripe peaches, but others need a peeler instead.

Pineapple shells are so hard that a heavy carving knife with serrated or scalloped edge is the safest instrument to use for removing the thorny crown and quartering the fruit lengthwise. Wear a rubber glove or protect your hand with a dishcloth, laying the fruit on its side, and grasping the crown to cut it off. A grapefruit knife with curved blade is best for removing the core and the fruit from the shell.

# Herbs and Spices

Dried herbs and spices should have distinctive aromas and good color for their varieties. If green herbs have darkened appreciably, turned gray, or lost their characteristic scent, they're old, lacking in flavor and should be discarded. Old herbs and spices won't spoil preserves and pickles, but they will make mild, less flavorful products. Dried whole-leaf herbs such as tarragon release their full scent and flavor only when crushed. To test, place about $1/4$ teaspoon of the herb in the palm of one hand, crumble the leaves between thumb and forefinger of your other hand, and smell the powder.

You will save time later on if you date each new container of herbs or spices before putting it away. Many are old after six months, but some will retain their strength as long as a year if they are stored in tightly covered, lightproof containers in a cool, dark spot.

# Salt

A couple of generations ago, pickling salt, which is a little coarser than table salt, was sold in virtually all groceries, even in cities. With the rebirth of interest in home canning, it may again become easy to find everywhere. However, I have given measurements for pickling and uniodized table salt as interchangeable, and for coarse (kosher) salt, which is twice as bulky as table salt and almost twice as bulky as pickling salt. Iodized salt can be used in any recipe that does not contain cucumbers. It won't affect the flavor of cucumber pickles, but the iodine can turn them dark. Reduced-sodium salt mixture should not be used; its sodium content is insufficient for safe pickling by the open kettle method, and it will not make crisp pickles.

## Water

If the area in which you live has hard water, it will have to be specially treated to prevent its natural mineral content from darkening pickles and interfering with the pickling process. To do this, simply boil the water that you are going to use for brine. Let it cool, then strain through four thicknesses of clean, dry cheesecloth and add white or cider vinegar in the ratio of 1 tablespoon per quart of water.

## Rock Candy Versus Sugar

Rock candy is refined sugar that undergoes additional refining by recrystallization. It was used as a medicine until the middle of the eighteenth century and is still favored by some people as a soothing remedy for a sore throat. It is called for in several of my beverage recipes largely for convenience. I have made the same drinks with granulated sugar with no apparent difference in flavor or appearance. But sugar tends to settle, so the mixture has to be stirred or shaken every day or two until the sugar has dissolved completely. This is not necessary with rock candy strings, which dissolve rapidly and evenly, leaving only a few small strings to be removed before you bottle the drinks. Rock candy is widely available at fancy food stores, candy stores, and even some drugstores. The brown variety, which is less

plentiful, usually can be found in stores catering to Chinese cus-
tomers.

# *Measuring Ingredients*

I have tried as often as possible to quote measurements by weight
for ingredients ordinarily sold that way, because few things are as ag-
gravating as the belated discovery that you have bought too little or
too much of something. I have also tried to avoid the use of small,
medium, and large as the sole definition of amount to buy, even for
ingredients such as citrus fruit, which usually sell by the piece rather
than the pound. An orange that looks small to me may look medium
or even large to someone else. It is easy to check the weight of produce in most stores; in many communities, markets are required by
law to provide scales.

I have made exceptions to this rule, however, in recipes that call
for sweet bell peppers, pineapples, and other types of produce whose
edible portion tends to vary widely from piece to piece. In recipes

using them, I have indicated both the approximate amount to buy and expected edible yield.

Measuring different types of ingredients is easier with the right utensils. Liquids can be gauged more accurately in a glass or plastic measure with a pouring lip. Dry ingredients such as sugar and salt are best measured in graduated metal or plastic cups so you can level the top with the cutting edge of a knife blade. A large (at least 1-quart) measure can be used for gauging the amount of fruits and vegetables after they're sliced, diced, chopped, or whatever, but I find a mixing bowl of at least 2- or 3-quart capacity is easier to use, provided it has either cup or avoirdupois (half-pint, pint, quart, and so on) markings on its sides.

# *Measurements and Equivalents*

Pinch = as much as can be picked up between thumb and index finger
⅓ tablespoon = 1 teaspoon

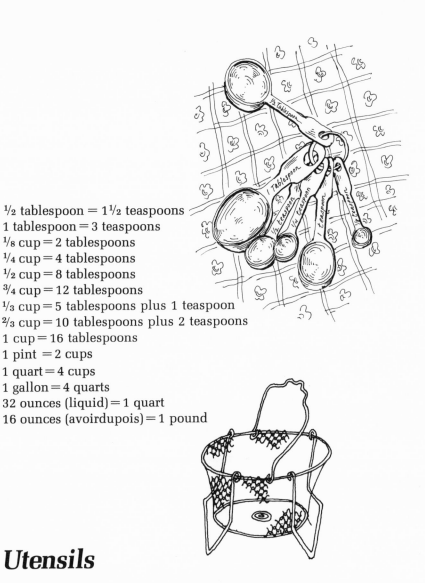

½ tablespoon = 1½ teaspoons
1 tablespoon = 3 teaspoons
⅛ cup = 2 tablespoons
¼ cup = 4 tablespoons
½ cup = 8 tablespoons
¾ cup = 12 tablespoons
⅓ cup = 5 tablespoons plus 1 teaspoon
⅔ cup = 10 tablespoons plus 2 teaspoons
1 cup = 16 tablespoons
1 pint = 2 cups
1 quart = 4 cups
1 gallon = 4 quarts
32 ounces (liquid) = 1 quart
16 ounces (avoirdupois) = 1 pound

# Utensils

Only a few basic utensils are necessary for small-scale preserving and pickling. You probably have most of them in your kitchen already. I have divided the list into two parts: the first consists of essentials; the second, of optional articles that can make your work faster and/or easier.

ESSENTIAL

Sterilizer (an 8-quart Dutch oven with tight-fitting cover is
    adequate)
Saucepans

Mixing bowls

A large slotted metal spoon

A large metal spoon with solid bowl

Eyedropper

Wooden spoons reserved only for preserving or pickling (those
    you use for general cooking sometimes retain odors and flavors)

Jar lifter or tongs (see source list, page 201)

Colander or large, fine-meshed strainer

Graduated measuring spoons, preferably a 6-unit set that includes
    measures for ⅛ teaspoon and ½ tablespoon

Graduated measuring cups

Food grinder, manual or electric

Heatproof glass measuring cups, preferably a 1-cup and a 1-quart
    size

Chopping board

Small, sharp, stainless steel paring knife

Stainless steel kitchen knife with 6- or 7-inch blade for chopping

Carving knife with serrated blade

Swivel-blade vegetable peeler

Reamer or electric juicer

Food mill or electric blender

Jelly bag or clean cheesecloth

Jar funnel

Grater with assorted size holes

Jars, glasses, paraffin, and labels

Scales—kitchen, diet, postal or bathroom (listed in order of
    preference)

# OPTIONAL

Collapsible wire salad basket with bucket handle
Cake or pot racks
Cherry pitter, plunger type

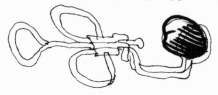

Potato masher
Berry huller, tweezer type
Long-handled rubber spatula
Tea strainer
Metal tea ball
Candy or deep-fry thermometer, preferably spoon type
Aluminum marking guide, the kind sold in sewing
  supply departments
Small melon ball cutter
Spring-operated steel and plastic chopper
Warming tray, electric

You will notice that many recipes warn against using aluminum
mixing bowls for brining ingredients. No safety factor is involved, but
salt that is allowed to stand in aluminum utensils can pit their sur-

face. Heavy gauge aluminum saucepans make excellent preserving and pickling kettles, provided they are used only for cooking and not for presoaking. Discoloration in aluminum pans is caused by mineral deposits naturally present in water. Acid foods (tomatoes, for instance) cooked in such pans will remove the discoloration harmlessly.

I recommend the use of stainless steel knives for a similar reason. Onions and some other ingredients discolor carbon steel blades and transfer the discoloration to food cut with them. Sharp blades are essential; dull blades lead to accidents because they tend to slip on hard produce instead of cutting it cleanly.

# Pots and Pans

Few recipes in this book require a saucepan larger than 4 quarts, and many can be cooked in a 2½-quart pan. The shape as well as the size is important. Straight-sided heavy gauge pans are best, both for stirring and for measuring the depth when a recipe must be boiled to reduce it by half.

The diameter is important, too. If you use a narrower pan than a recipe calls for, you'll need extra cooking time because of the smaller surface for evaporation.

Smaller capacity pans should not be used because the contents might boil over.

It may help you adjust cooking times if you know the capacity and the diameter of the pans I used in testing the recipes:

| CAPACITY | DIAMETER (MEASURED INSIDE TOP RIM) |
|---|---|
| 1 quart | 5¾ inches |
| 1½ quarts | 6 inches |
| 2 quarts | 7 inches |
| 2½ quarts | 8 inches |
| 4 quarts | 8 inches |
| 8 quarts | 10½ inches |

A 4-quart pressure cooker without its lid is ideal for any recipe needing a pan of that capacity. Heavy gauge aluminum or steel Dutch ovens also work well, but uncoated iron pots never should be used because they can darken some mixtures and form dangerous chemicals when certain acid foods are cooked in them. Iron pans also are dangerously heavy to pour from — and some recipes, such as jellies, are easier to pour than they are to ladle or spoon into jars.

Lightweight, very thin aluminum utensils are just as unsuitable. Jams, jellies, preserves, marmalades — in fact, any mixture containing a lot of sugar — can stick and burn in thin pans almost before you scent trouble.

If your kitchen range is electric, be sure the pan you use fits the burner, to ensure even cooking and conservation of energy. This is less of a problem with gas ranges, as heat can be adjusted instantly to cover the base of the pan.

Even if you use the size pan called for in each recipe, cooking times can vary because of the differing pectin and water content of fruits and vegetables, and the altitude. For every 1,000 feet above sea level, cooking time must be increased. Your Cooperative Extension Agent or local utility company home economist can provide details. Again, it may help you to know that the produce I used for testing the recipes was grown during an exceptionally rainy year. The pectin content should be higher, and the water content lower, in fruits and vegetables of a drier season.

# Jars and Glasses

The ideal container for most preserving and pickling is a home canning, or Mason, jar with a threaded neck and a self-sealing lid. It is made to withstand the high temperatures and pressures of both water-bath and pressure canning as well as open kettle preserving. The jar can be reused indefinitely if it is handled carefully to avoid scratching and cracking. Incidentally, the John L. Mason for whom the jars are named did not invent them; but in 1858, when he was only twenty-six

years old, he patented an improved thread and an improved mold for blowing bottles with threaded necks. Mason, a New Yorker, was one of many people who patented fruit jars and closures in the middle of the nineteenth century. His inventions succeeded because they produced an airtight seal, and the popularity of home canning, preserving, and pickling dates from his time.

To repeat, the Mason jar is ideal, but commercial canning jars that mayonnaise, pickles, peanut butter, and baby and junior foods come in can be used safely for some types of preserving. These containers are suitable for anything that requires refrigerator or freezer storage or that can be sealed with melted paraffin. Most jams, jellies, preserves, and marmalades fall into the latter class. It is important always to have the surface smooth. If it is lumpy, a thick or uneven layer of paraffin will be necessary and the contents are liable to leak during storage.

Standard Mason jars are preferred for water bath processing, and are absolutely necessary for safe pressure canning. But pint and quart mayonnaise jars can be used for water bath processing if they are free from scratches and chips. It is extremely important that new two-part Mason jar lids be substituted for the paper-lined lids that come with the jars. The two-part lids also are necessary for open kettle preserving and pickling, to provide a vacuum seal.

Instant coffee jars in odd shapes make interesting containers for jelly. But be sure to fill them to the shoulder before you paraffin. Otherwise, the hardened wax will be difficult to remove.

Antique or old Mason jars are charming to look at but not, in my opinion, safe for general use in preserving and pickling. There is no way to tell when and if a perfect seal has been achieved with a rubber ring–glass lid–wire hinge closure or with a rubber ring and glass-lined zinc lid. So I reserve jars with such closures for icebox pickles and brandied fruits and beverages, which require no vacuum seal for safe storage.

## *Decorative Containers*

Apothecary jars with ground glass, plastic, or cork stoppers make attractive, practical containers for any preserved or pickled products that need refrigerator storage. They seal and reseal tightly, and the ground glass and cork stoppers can be sterilized by boiling (whereas plastic tops must be scalded). This kind of jar can also be used for fruits in port, which can be stored safely at room temperature.

Footed, dishwasher-safe glassware — such as balloon brandy glasses, parfaits, wine glasses, and goblets — makes attractive containers for gift jellies and marmalades. But such glasses must be handled gently to avoid damage while scalding or packing. Like commercial canning jars, they cool quickly and break more readily than standard home-canning, or Mason, jars and glasses.

# Safety

It is important that all jars be hot when you pack them with hot food. Otherwise, they can break and cause a nasty burn as well as waste all the good food. The commercial canning jars and the decorative containers that I have described are especially vulnerable because they are thinner than the Mason jars made especially for home canning, preserving, and pickling. When I use the thinner-walled containers, I remove them from the sterilizer one at a time and fill each one before removing the next.

To repeat, most commercial and decorative containers never should be used to pack anything that requires water bath or pressure processing. Even the mayonnaise jars that can be used cautiously for water bath processing are unsafe for pressure canning. They are not tempered to withstand the high temperatures and stress and, as a result, could explode. Even if the jars look perfect, do not risk it. Invisible scratches or cracks can be caused by rough handling during shipment or at home. Just scraping out the contents with a spoon can leave a scratch that could trigger an explosion during water bath or pressure canning. In addition, some commercial jars lack the depth of band necessary to get a vacuum seal with home-canning lids.

# Lids

Mason jars come with self-sealing lids and directions for using them. Replacement lids—the tops alone or rings (bands) with tops—also come with directions for use (on or in the boxes in which they are packed in quantities of twelve). Jelly glasses come with metal or plastic snap-on lids to be used after the paraffin seal has solidified and the glasses have cooled.

Lids from commercial jars that pickles or olives were packed in tend to retain odors which can be removed easily and naturally, without resorting to either smelly chemicals or all-purpose cleaning agents. Wash, scald, and dry the lids as usual, then set them, upside down, on a sunny windowsill for several days until all the odor has disappeared. Wash and dry them again before using.

# Removing Labels

More and more manufacturers are using self-stick jar labels. They are less difficult to remove if you pull off as much as you can before washing the jars. Hot water tends to set the adhesive. Residual glue from labels can be removed with cotton pads soaked with either liquid spot remover or lighter fluid. But both these solvents are flammable, so they never should be used near a range or a hot plate or by anyone who is smoking. A 4-ounce bottle of spot remover will remove dozens of labels. Some such products leave an oily film that must be washed off with very hot, soapy water. Lighter fluid requires even more scrubbing than cleaning fluid, and it tends to evaporate faster.

Nail polish remover, which is also flammable, will remove some types of glue, but its perfumed smell is almost as hard to remove as the glue itself.

# Sterilizing or Scalding Containers

Before you prepare ingredients for a recipe, assemble jars and/or glasses, lids, canning funnel, and paraffin. Run a finger around the rims and threads of jars, and discard any with cracks or scratches that would prevent a perfect seal. Do not reuse lids of the two-part type, and reuse bands only if they are undented and free from rust. Stores that sell Mason jars usually also sell boxes of replacement lids and cap (ring) and lid combinations, twelve to the box.

Wash the jars, glasses, and lids in hot, soapy water. If the jars and glasses are going to be used for preserves and other spreads, they need not be sterilized, but they should be scalded with boiling water and they must be kept hot so they will not crack or break when you fill them. I find the easiest way to do this is to place the scalded containers in hot water in the pot you are using as a sterilizer and cover it. Containers to be sterilized should be rinsed well and placed in a large, tightly covered pan, preferably one that is deep enough to hold all of them in an upright position. If you have to place jars or glasses on their sides, they are harder to remove when hot, and fewer can be sterilized at one time. Fill each container with an inch or two of cold water and the bottom of the sterilizer with about the same depth of water. Some people like to put a folded clean towel or a shallow rack in the sterilizer to keep the glasses from rattling, but I find the water in them works as effectively. If there is room, place the canning funnel with or on top of one of the jars and cover the sterilizer tightly.

About 20 to 30 minutes before the food is ready to pack, bring the water in the sterilizer to a boil over medium heat. When steam emerges, lower the heat so the water boils steadily for at least 15 minutes.

About 15 minutes before the food is ready to pack, place the washed, rinsed lids, jar lifter or tongs, packing spoon or ladle, and a table knife in an open saucepan with water deep enough to cover the lids, the tong tips, the spoon bowl, and the knife blade. Boil 5 minutes, timing from the moment when vigorous bubbling begins. Leave them in the water until needed.

If the food isn't quite ready when the jars and utensils are, turn off the heat under the sterilizer and utensils and let them stand, covered, until the containers are needed. As long as they are hot, they are safe to use. If they cool off before the food is ready, simply reheat them briefly.

# Packing and Sealing

To remove a container from the sterilizer with a jar lifter or tongs, grasp a jar just below its threaded neck and other containers around their widest point. (Do not let tongs touch the sterile interiors of the containers.) Hold the lifter or tongs firmly as you tilt the container to empty water from it into the sterilizer. Gently place the container, right side up, on a metal rack or wooden surface or a folded towel — never on a solid metal surface that could cause breakage. Leave at least one inch of space between containers so they will cool evenly. Keep them out of drafts. Sudden temperature changes, such as a direct draft from an air conditioner, can crack or break a boiling hot jar.

You should pack everything except pickled and brandied fruits and certain vegetable pickles one jar at a time, sealing each jar before the next is removed from the sterilizer. Exceptions to this rule are explained in individual recipes.

When you pack pickled fruit and other foods whose syrup or brine must be boiling hot or boiled to the syrupy stage, line up all the sterilized containers at once, pack with solids in rapid succession and cover lightly with a clean dish towel or paper toweling to keep out dust and other contaminants while you finish cooking the liquid. Use a slotted spoon to drain excess liquid from the jars and leave about ¾ to 1 inch of head space to allow for expansion of the solids as they cool. If the recipe directs, bring the syrup to a boil and boil it rapidly until reduced to desired thickness. Unless a recipe directs otherwise, fill jars almost to overflowing with syrup or brine. In any case, make sure the solids are completely covered by liquid. Whole fruit and large pieces of fruit tend to float. Fruits such as peaches and pears darken unappetizingly when they're not covered by liquid. To prevent this, top the fruit with a crumpled piece of parchment paper before sealing each jar if the jar is to be sealed while hot. Waxed paper can be substituted for parchment paper in brandied fruits or other preserves that must be cooled before sealing, but aluminum foil or plastic wrap will not do. Too little is known about possible chemical reaction with the hot syrups.

Always spoon, ladle, or pour preserved foods as close to the rim of the jar or glass as possible to prevent air bubbles from forming. Any that do form should be released by running a clean, scalded knife blade between the food and the walls of the jar.

If you want to paraffin a marmalade that sets slowly, let it stand, lightly covered with a clean towel, until the surface is firm enough to support a thin layer of melted paraffin.

Most relishes, conserves, chutneys, and cooked pickles should be left over very low heat to keep warm while you pack jars one at a time. I generally set a small rack or chopping board beside the burner to hold each jar as I pack it.

Some jams, jellies, preserves, and marmalades begin setting quickly, so it is a good idea to line up all the hot containers for them at once and pack them in rapid succession before cleaning and sealing.

As jars cool, you may hear sharp, popping sounds. The noise signals that the lids are sealing automatically and creating a vacuum that helps preserve the food. Follow each manufacturer's directions for testing for seal, and do not worry if all the lids fail to seal at once. Some take twelve or more hours. Sometimes a lid that has not sealed automatically will do so when you touch it lightly with a finger. If it does, and then stays down, the seal is safe. Any food in jars that fail to seal should be used promptly or reheated and repacked.

# Paraffining

Paraffin can be melted in any heatproof container, but it should *never* be placed on direct heat. It is a petroleum product that blazes at a relatively low temperature, and it should always be melted over indirect heat. Either set your melter in a pan of hot water over very low heat or, better yet, on an electric warming tray with the control, if any, at its lowest setting. If you have no such tray, place the paraffin container in an inch or so of water in a skillet over low heat and return the container to the skillet between uses.

For years, I have used a small, cheap aluminum teapot as my paraffin melter and storage container. I clean the outside occasionally but never bother cleaning inside because the lid keeps out dust. And I plug the spout, during storage, with rolled paper toweling. By keeping the pot solely for paraffin, I avoid the aggravation of cleaning solid wax off a utensil needed for other purposes. The spout makes the melted wax easy to pour, and it also helps prevent dribbles. Because the top opening is small, the paraffin cakes must be cut or broken to fit. It is easy to do if you place one cake of paraffin at a time on a wooden cutting surface and score it deeply with a small, sharp knife. Then you can break it easily with your hands.

I also recycle used paraffin. After rinsing the solid rounds under hot water, I let them dry completely and drop them back into the teapot.

Before you paraffin any jelly or preserve, make sure the inner rim of its container is clean and dry. Steam or a drop of jelly will prevent a tight seal so that mold can develop during storage. I have found after considerable trial and error that I can keep the inside rim clear if I first fill the jar or glass within 1 inch of the top, clean that inch with a paper towel wrung out in hot water, and then carefully pour in more jelly to fill within 1/4 inch of the top.

Always pour melted paraffin slowly and let it spread naturally over the hot surface until it is about 1/8 inch thick. Tilt each glass gently to spread the wax to all the edges. When the wax has hardened, it will turn white. Let the preserve reach room temperature, then add a second paraffin layer the same depth as the first. A single thick layer is liable to leak during long storage.

# Storage

When the second layer of paraffin is firm, clean the outside of the jar, cover with its lid; label and date, and store in a cool, dark, dry spot. The same steps should be followed for food packed in jars with two-part, glass, or glass-lined zinc lids. If you have no cool storage area — and I don't mean the refrigerator — use only jars with self-sealing two-part lids. Warmth, humidity, and/or the heat that comes with light can make preserves weep and seep through a paraffin seal. When this happens, the contents can mold. Of course, preserves you plan to use within a few weeks can always be paraffined safely. During prolonged storage, most spreads tend to lose flavor and quality. Unless a recipe indicates otherwise, use them within six months.

# Fading and Darkening

Fruits, especially the red ones, tend either to darken or to fade if they are left on a table or counter top or stored for long periods. The addition of ascorbic acid (vitamin C) or ascorbic acid mixture (sugar, vitamin C, and an anticaking agent) during preparation and canning helps retard color changes, but I have found nothing totally effective with raspberries, strawberries, peaches, rhubarb, and light-colored plums. Ascorbic acid is available at drugstores and health food stores. It is usually sold in tablet form and should be crushed before using. Ascorbic acid mixture usually is widely available at supermarkets in areas where a lot of canning and preserving is done, and it can sometimes be found in drugstores in urban areas. If you cannot locate a supplier in your community, write the manufacturer (see source list, page 201). Follow the manufacturer's directions for using the mixture if you use a brand other than the one indicated in the source list.

If you use crystalline ascorbic acid, sprinkle ¼ teaspoon on the contents of pint jars or ½ teaspoon on contents of quart jars just before sealing them. If you cannot obtain the crystalline form, crush ascorbic acid tablets and sprinkle the equivalent of 125 milligrams on the contents of pint jars (or 250 milligrams for quarts).

# *Open Kettle Versus Water Bath Packing*

There is a current trend toward using the water bath method for pickling and preserving many foods that used to be packed by the open kettle method. The old-fashioned open kettle system works this way: you cook the ingredients until done in an uncovered saucepan, pack them, boiling hot, into hot, sterilized jars, and seal each jar as soon as it is filled (exceptions are noted in individual recipes, in which syrup has to be reduced by boiling after hot fruit is in the jars). This method is safe for all acid fruits and vegetables if they are packed in syrup that uses enough sugar or honey or corn syrup or combinations of two or more of these sweeteners, or in brine that is either very salty or made with a large quantity of full-strength — 4 to 6 percent — vinegar.

The open kettle method that I have used and recommend throughout the book rarely leads to spoilage if you follow directions exactly, work quickly (which is easy because the batches are small), and keep your hands and all your jars, utensils, work surfaces, and ingredients scrupulously clean.

However, if you live in a hot, humid climate and have neither air conditioning nor a cool, dry cellar for storage, follow the recommendations of your County Cooperative Extension Agent for the high-temperature water bath method for packing pickles, chutneys, and other relishes, fruit butters, conserves, jams, preserves, and fruits in sugar syrup without liquor or brandy. Those containing liquor or brandy must be allowed to cool before the alcoholic beverage is added if you want the sugar to be converted into alcohol by fermentation. The water bath method is always necessary for preserving with reduced quantities of sugar and vinegar. The boiling or simmering water supplies enough heat to destroy bacteria, enzymes, yeasts, and molds that can spoil even acid foods.

Pressure canning creates an even higher temperature (240 degrees Fahrenheit), which is necessary for safe packing of all low acid foods—canned vegetables, meat, fish, poultry, and seafood, for instance. But I am not concerned with such foods in this book.

Information about both water bath and pressure canning is obtainable from:

Jar and lid manufacturers' booklets, which can be ordered for minimal sums.

U.S. Department of Agriculture booklets: *How to Make Jellies, Jams and Preserves at Home* (G56); *Making Pickles and Relishes at Home* (G92). (Single copies are free from the Office of Information, U.S. Department of Agriculture, Washington, D.C. 20250. Order by number, not title, and include your Zip Code.)

Cooperative Extension Agents are in every county in the United States. They usually are listed under that name in the white pages of the telephone book and also under the names of state agricultural colleges and land grant universities.

# Spoilage

One thing that can spoil any home-packed product is a bad spot left on food when you prepare it. Bruises on cucumbers can lead to soft, rotten pickles. Pick your fruit and vegetables carefully, and trim away bruised or moldy areas if they are small. If they are large, discard the piece of fruit or vegetable entirely rather than risk spoiling a whole batch of preserves or pickles. When I have to use packaged instead of loose produce, I always buy a little extra to make up for possible loss. Some varieties of fruit are especially susceptible to hidden spoilage. In individual recipes calling for them, I have mentioned this hazard and recommended buying a larger quantity than is actually needed for the recipe.

Mold sometimes attacks both preserves sealed with paraffin and sour or brined pickles that are not completely covered with liquid. These pickles should always be discarded without tasting. So should moldy preserves, according to the latest advice from the U.S. Department of Agriculture. For years the Department considered preserves (and jams, jellies and marmalades) safe to eat if the mold content was scanty and removable and the spread smelled and looked normal, but they are obviously being more cautious now.

Most preserves and related spreads in opened but covered containers keep well at room temperature if they are served every day or so and used completely within a few weeks. If resealed jars are left that way for long periods at warm room temperatures, the contents tend to mold. Refrigeration helps prevent this, but if you eat preserves only occasionally, the quality as well as the shelf life will be better if you pack them in containers just large enough for a few servings.

If pickles become slippery to touch or develop an off-odor, discard them without tasting and in such a way that neither humans nor pets can get at them. Most pickles in opened jars keep satisfactorily at cool room temperature under the same conditions as preserves, but they generally taste better when chilled. Crispness is more pronounced, especially with dills, bread-and-butter pickles, and almost any pickles that are packed in sweet-and-sour syrup.

# Altering Recipes

All the recipes in this book can be doubled, but you will get better results if you follow my directions for small batches.

As I suggested earlier, the quality of preserves and pickles remains higher if they are packed in containers that hold only enough food for two or three meals. Once a jar is opened, the flavor and the color of food left in it gradually deteriorate.

Many recipes can be halved without difficulty. It is especially simple to divide the ingredients for recipes meant to be cooked in two batches, although you may have to use a little more than half the seasonings in a divided recipe. Do rely on your personal taste in this area, but remember that most pickles and relishes mellow and lose their sharpness when they are permitted to stand for a few weeks in a cool, dark spot.

IMPORTANT

Most preserved and pickled foods with reduced acidity or sweetness require special processing, storage, and handling to avoid spoilage that can lead to food poisoning in general and deadly botulism poisoning in particular. Botulin toxin thrives in low-acid food in an airless environment such as that of a vacuum sealed canning jar.

To avoid this risk, never reduce the amount of vinegar in a recipe that is too tart for your taste. Add sugar or corn syrup or honey instead.

Never reduce the amount of salt in a brine.

If you want to reduce sweetness or replace sugar with a noncaloric or low-calorie substitute, either use recipes developed especially for these purposes or consult your county Cooperative Extension Agent for directions for converting specific recipes to a high-temperature method of processing. Special storage and handling may also be necessary. Agents usually are listed by title in the white pages of the telephone directory. If your community does not have a Cooperative Extension Agent, ask the consumer service department of your local public utility (gas and electric company) for the address of the nearest one.

Sources for low-sugar or sugar-free recipes include manufacturers of sugar substitutes, whose addresses can be found on their product packages.

# Timing

Timing is flexible in recipes that call for a mixture to stand anywhere from a few hours to 24 or more. A difference of an hour or two will not ruin your pickles or preserves. Of course, in very hot weather or in an unusually warm kitchen, you should refrigerate unfinished mixtures to keep them from fermenting if you must hold them much longer than a recipe suggests.

Overcooking or undercooking can be more troublesome. Overcooked fruit spreads may become cloudy, sticky, rubbery, dark, tough, or even caramelized. Some preserving mixtures made without added pectin can be recooked briefly if they aren't quite thick enough or have not set, but some will darken unappetizingly during the second cooking. Rather than risk this, I usually serve too-thin preserves at refrigerator temperature, which thickens them a little, or use them as sauces for desserts, pancakes, waffles, or French toast.

Overcooked pickles and relishes become mushy, and some darken badly. Undercooked ones can be reheated without risk, but remember that crispness is one of the most desirable qualities in a good pickle product.

# The Pectin Puzzle

Pectin is the substance in fruits and berries that combines with sugar to make jellies, jams, preserves, and marmalades jell. The amount of pectin varies according to the species of fruit or berry, its degree of ripeness, and even growing conditions. A wet season produces juicy fruit with low pectin content. A dry season creates less juice but more pectin.

However, in almost all the recipes that follow, the variables are not significant enough for you to bother about testing pectin and acid content, and you can rely on the proportions I have worked out, except in the instances where I have indicated a test is necessary. And, of course, it is important to know how to determine acid and pectin levels when you start to improvise and create your own preserves.

Both pectin and acid are needed in minimum amounts for jelling. Many recipes that predate the invention of commercial pectin call for two or more varieties of fruit to get enough jelling strength. It is also possible to step up the pectin content with homemade lemon pectin extract (page 40), apple pectin extract (page 39), or liquefied powdered pectin (page 44). Acid content can be increased by adding lemon juice. Before testing for either pectin or acid, boil the juice at least 5 minutes. The pectin content of uncooked juice will not register.

*Acid test:* Taste a spoonful to see if the juice is as tart as a mixture of one part fresh lemon juice diluted with three parts water. If it is not, add ½ to 1 tablespoon of fresh lemon juice for each cup of jelly stock or fruit mixture.

*Pectin test:* There are four methods for gauging pectin level. One uses a device called a jelmeter, which is not widely distributed and is hardly worth seeking out unless you plan to do a great deal of preserving. Another involves boiling ¼ cup of unsweetened juice rapidly with 2½ tablespoons of sugar until the mixture glazes the tines of a fork and forms droplets on the tines when the fork is held vertically. If the jelly starts to caramelize or darken before the mixture passes the jell test, more pectin or pectin extract should be added to the jelly stock before cooking the whole recipe. You can waste a lot of fruit and juice this way, so I never use the cooking test. Nor do I bother with the third test, which uses a combination of sugar and epsom salts and requires a 20-minute wait for results.

The fourth test, which is the quickest and easiest, uses tiny amounts of fruit juice and grain alcohol (grain neutral spirits, the alcoholic base for whiskey, gin, vodka, and other liquors) or poisonous isopropyl alcohol, which is widely available in drugstores as rubbing alcohol with 70 percent alcoholic content. This test can be made in one minute, literally. You'll find directions for it in the Basic Jelly or Marmalade recipe that follows:

*Grain or rubbing alcohol*
*Cooked, strained fruit juice or a mixture of*
  *cooked fruit and juice*
*Lemon pectin extract (page 40) or apple pectin*
  *extract (page 39) or liquefied powdered*
  *pectin (page 44) or bottled pectin*
*Sugar*
*Flavoring (optional)*

*Test for pectin:* Measure 1 teaspoon of 190-proof grain alcohol or 70 percent rubbing alcohol into a clean, dry cup. If juice to be tested is still warm, use a clean, dry spoon to scoop up 1 teaspoon of the juice, and rest the spoon atop an ice cube to cool the juice quickly. Stir it gently into the alcohol and let stand at least 1 minute. Then, pour the mixture gently onto a clean, dry saucer. If a solid mass of gelatin forms (this rarely happens), the pectin level is high and you should allow 1 cup of sugar for each cup of juice or fruit and juice mixture. If large, broken flakes of gelatin form, the pectin level is moderately high—the ideal proportion—and you will need ⅔ to ¾ cup of sugar for each cup of juice (or fruit and juice combined). If the mixture remains liquid or if the gelatin flakes are small and sparse, either concentrate the pectin by boiling the juice (or fruit and juice) mixture 10 to 20 minutes or add one of the extracts or liquefied powdered pectin or bottled pectin in the following proportions. (But before proceeding, discard each test mixture without tasting. This is particularly important when you use poisonous rubbing alcohol. Keep both types away from your kitchen range and lighted cigarettes — alcohol fumes are highly flammable. Be sure to cap the bottle tightly when not in use.) Measure 1 cup of juice (or juice-fruit mixture) into a 1-pint measure or bowl. Stir in 4 to 6 tablespoons of either pectin extract or ½ to 1 tablespoon of liquefied powdered pectin or bottled pectin.

Using 1 teaspoon of this fortified mixture, make the pectin test again. If results show the ideal moderate pectin level, then measure the remaining juice (or juice-fruit mixture) and follow the same formula, adding as much pectin extract or liquefied powdered pectin or bottled pectin per cup as indicated.

If you have concentrated the pectin by boiling the juice (or fruit-juice mixture) instead, make the pectin test again to determine how much sugar per cup is needed.

After you have fortified the pectin level of all the juice or fruit-juice mixture, either stir in the required amount of sugar until no crystals are visible or measure 3 cups of the unsweetened juice or fruit-juice into a wide 2½-quart saucepan and the required amount of sugar into a bowl. Bring the juice to boil quickly, stir in the sugar all at once, and boil the mixture rapidly until jell tests done. To prevent overcooking, remove the pan from heat each time you test for jell. Cook remaining juice or fruit-juice mixture in small batches.

A chart rating fruit for pectin and acid content can only be approximate, because of weather fluctuations and other influences described earlier. Keep this in mind as you choose ingredients from the following lists:

### FRUIT HIGH IN PECTIN AND ACID

| | |
|---|---|
| Apples, sour | Lemons |
| Cranberries | Limes |
| Currants, red | Oranges, sour or Seville |
| Grapefruit | Plums, sour |
| Grapes, Concord and wild | Quinces, unripe |

### FRUIT HIGH IN PECTIN, LOW IN ACID

| | |
|---|---|
| Apples, sweet | Oranges, sweet |
| Blueberries | Plums, clingstone, sweet |
| Cherries, sweet | Quinces, ripe |
| Crabapples | Tangerines |

### FRUIT HIGH IN ACID, LOW IN PECTIN

| | |
|---|---|
| Apricots, fresh and dried | Rhubarb |
| Cherries, sour | Strawberries, ripe and unripe |
| Pineapple, ripe and unripe | |

### FRUIT LOW IN ACID AND PECTIN

| | |
|---|---|
| Bananas | Pears |
| Nectarines | Raspberries |
| Peaches | All overripe fruit |

# Pectin Extracts

The apple variety of pectin extract is simply a concentrate of apple jelly made from tart, preferably underripe, fruit. If you make it from sweet apples, you may need to add lemon juice for acidity, in the ratio indicated on page 35. Citrus pectin extracts can be made from lemons, oranges, or grapefruit. I find lemon the most useful. Both apple and lemon pectin extracts are based on recipes in a Louisiana State Extension Service booklet, whose authors suggest using a 15-minute water bath for any extracts that will not be used immediately.

However, I have stored both extracts for months, including even the summer, after packing them by the open kettle method. Both also freeze well, and can be thawed at room temperature. If you freeze them, leave 1 inch of head space in each jar to allow for expansion.

# Apple Pectin Extract

4 pounds sliced, unpeeled apples, tart, firm
  ones such as greenings in winter or Granny
  Smiths in summer
2 quarts water

🍓 Wash and dry apples. Remove stems and slice apples, including peels and cores, into a straight-sided wide 4-quart saucepan. Add water, cover tightly, bring to boil, and boil 20 minutes. Strain and measure juice. You should have about 6 cups.

(If you like apple butter, reserve the pulp, purée it to remove seeds and skin, mix it with ⅔ cup of sugar for each cup of strained purée, season to taste with ground cinnamon, cloves, and nutmeg, and cook until thick, stirring often, to prevent sticking and burning. The yield will vary.)

Wash and dry the saucepan, return juice to it, and measure depth. Boil the juice, uncovered, until reduced by half. Drip the juice through a clean jelly bag wrung out in hot water or two thicknesses of dampened cheesecloth. Do not squeeze. The pomace (pulp) remaining can be added to the apple butter mixture before cooking, if desired.

Refrigerate extract in a clean, tightly covered container if you plan to use it within a few days. For longer storage, heat it to boiling in a 1-quart saucepan, pack in hot, sterilized half-pint jars, and seal. Makes about 3 cups.

# Lemon Pectin Extract

Seeds and coarsely ground white pith of 5 to 6
   large, thick-skinned lemons, about 1 1/2
   pounds, or the equivalent weight in smaller
   lemons
3 tablespoons citric or tartaric acid (citric
   acid, made from citrus fruit and labeled sour
   salt, can be found in the spice rack at most
   supermarkets; tartaric acid, made from
   grapes, is sold by wine supply shops)
6 quarts water

🌿 With a swivel-blade peeler, remove and discard the zest (shiny yellow outer peel) from the lemons, but do not cut deeply — the pectin is in the white pith beneath the zest. It won't matter if the peeled fruit is tinged a pale yellow.

Squeeze the lemons, reserving seeds, pulp, and pith. (I usually sweeten the juice and freeze it to make lemonade later.) Grind the pulp and pith coarsely, and measure. You should have about 2 cups, packed. Place this, the seeds, 1 tablespoon of the citric or tartaric acid, and 2 quarts of water in a straight-sided 4-quart saucepan. Let stand, uncovered, at least 2 hours, then measure the depth of the pan's contents and make a note of it. (An aluminum marking guide for home sewing is good for measuring because it can be scalded or sterilized.)

Bring the mixture to boil over medium heat, stirring often to prevent sticking. Boil rapidly until it is reduced by half. Stir often toward the end of the cooking period, which will take at least an hour or more. When the depth measures half the original figure, pour the extract through a strainer or colander lined with 4 thicknesses of damp cheesecloth into a bowl of at least 2-quart capacity.

Return the pomace (pulp) to the saucepan, add another tablespoon of citric or tartaric acid and 2 more quarts of water, and measure and cook as you did the first batch. No presoaking is necessary for this or the third and final batch. The second and third batches tend to reduce more rapidly than the first. Strain each batch when done into the first one.

When you strain the third batch, squeeze the pomace to extract as much liquid as possible. Put the extract through a clean, dampened jelly bag or two thicknesses of dampened cheesecloth, without squeezing. Let it drip several hours, until you have about 6 cups of cloudy liquid. If you plan to use it within a few days, refrigerate the extract in clean, tightly covered containers.

To store it for future use, bring extract to a boil in a 1½-quart saucepan, then pack, boiling hot, into hot, sterilized half-pint jars and seal. Store as you would jelly. Before using, always shake or stir the extract to mix in the sediment that settles during storage. Makes about 4½ cups.

# How to Make a Jelly Bag

Old-fashioned jelly bags, some with metal rings and stands, are sold at housewares shops and sometimes by mail order. I stopped using them when I discovered how much easier it is to make and maintain a cheesecloth substitute. Cut a large square of double-thick, clean cheesecloth. Wring it out in hot water so it will not absorb (and thus waste) juice, and use it to line a large colander or strainer set in a bowl. Pour in the cooked fruit mixture, and double-knot opposite corners of the cheesecloth to make two loops of about equal length. Suspend a bent wire hanger from a kitchen cabinet knob above a counter top, and suspend the improvised bag from the hanger by both loops. Make sure the bag is centered over the bowl. Remove the colander or strainer and let the juice drip into the bowl as indicated in the recipe. If you want clear jelly, do not squeeze the bag. When the dripping stops, remove the bag and either discard the pomace (pulp) or strain out seeds or pits and purée the pulp to make fruit butter.

Rinse the cheesecloth thoroughly in hot water, scald it, wring, and let dry. Store in a plastic bag until needed again, or throw it out and make a new bag each time.

# Jell Tests

There are three common and easy tests for doneness, or jell, in preserving. Most authorities consider the temperature test the most reliable one, but I have had consistently better results by using the sheet and refrigerator tests, double-checking one against the other. To avoid overcooking, always remove pan from heat while making any jell test.

*Temperature test:* Jelly and the liquid part of many marmalades and some preserves and jams jell at about 220 degrees Fahrenheit, which is 8 degrees above the point at which water boils at sea level. But differences in altitude and/or atmospheric pressure can raise or lower the temperature at which water boils, so it is advisable to check the boiling point shortly before you begin cooking any spread that should set like jelly.

To check boiling point, fill a small saucepan with enough water to cover your candy or deep-fry thermometer to the depth recommended by its manufacturer. When the water boils vigorously, read the temperature as the manufacturer recommends, make a note of that temperature, and cook the jelly until it registers 8 degrees above that temperature.

If you have a 4-cup flameproof glass percolator, you can learn to do the thermometer test quickly by boiling jelly or marmalade, about 3 cups at a time, in the pot with the insides removed. The percolator is deep enough to hold several different brands of dial-type thermometer at the correct level, and the pouring spout helps you develop a steady hand for filling glasses and jars.

*Sheet test:* Dip a small amount of boiling jelly up with a clean, cool, dry metal tablespoon, and either hold it about 12 inches above the pan, out of the steam, to cool slightly, or rest the bowl of the spoon a minute on a cool saucer nearby. Then tilt the spoon so the jelly runs off the side of its bowl. If it falls in two separate drops, the jelly needs more cooking. But if two drops merge and fall as one sheet, the jelly is done.

Incidentally, when making the sheet test, never use a spoon that has set jelly clinging to it or you may get a false positive. I keep a tall glass of cool water nearby to put the spoon in between tests so it cleans itself and cools off.

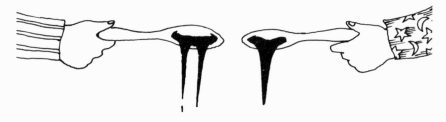

*Refrigerator test:* Jelly when done will also set lightly within a couple of minutes on a chilled saucer in the coolest part of the refrigerator. Do not be discouraged if jellies that test done by one or more of these methods remain syrupy in their glasses or jars for hours. When they are made without commercial pectin, some take as much as 24 hours to set firmly. And they should always be allowed to stand undisturbed until firm. This keeps the jell from breaking.

## Half-full Jars

Batches rarely come out even with the number of 8-ounce jars or glasses you prepare. If you are going to cook a second batch of jelly or other spread right away, cover any half-full container lightly with a clean paper towel or cloth so it will remain hot until more can be added from the second batch. If you end with a partly filled jar, just set it aside for immediate use or refrigerate it for use within a few weeks.

# Packaged and Bottled Pectins

Few recipes in this book use packaged (powdered) or bottled (liquid) pectin. For me, their disadvantages outweigh their advantages. Used as directed, both types of commercial pectin save time and effort, and they rarely fail to jell. But so much sugar is needed to make them work that a lot of fruit flavor is lost. Powdered fruit pectin has one other disadvantage—it makes a lot more jelly (or other spread) than most small families want. One package seldom makes fewer than eight medium glasses or jars, and it often yields as many as twelve to fifteen.

However, wine jellies and some herb jellies and low-pectin fruit spreads cannot be made without added pectin. I prefer the bottled type for wine jellies because homemade pectin extracts tend to impose their own flavors, changing the entire character of the spreads. I have used bottled pectin in one herb jelly and fresh lemons for another, but apple juice alone or apple pectin extract (page 39) combined with a low-pectin juice also makes a good base for herb flavors.

Keep in mind when you work with commercial pectins that the two types are not interchangeable unless a recipe gives specific directions.

For consistently perfect results, one brand of packaged pectin can be substituted for the other only if you liquefy it before adding it to the other ingredients. And even then, it should be used only in measured amounts, to fortify a low-pectin fruit mixture. For directions, see the Basic Jelly and Marmalade recipe (page 36).

Directions for liquefying a 2-ounce package of pectin are given in the product's recipe enclosure. To liquefy the contents of a 1¾-ounce package, measure ¾ cup of water into a 2-quart saucepan. Gradually sprinkle the pectin into the water, stirring constantly to prevent lumping. (Do not add water to pectin instead. This method forms lumps that no amount of beating will dissolve.) Bring to full, rolling boil over high heat, stirring constantly, and boil rapidly 1 minute, timing from the moment when full boil begins. Remove from heat, and either use at once or pack in a hot, scalded half-pint jar, seal, cool, and refrigerate. Makes about ¾ cup. I have kept it for as long as a month without loss of strength.

# Jams,
# Jellies, Preserves,
# Marmalades,
# and a Butter

# Concord Grape Jam

This may be the easiest recipe in the book, and one of the freshest tasting. Melted down with a little water, the jam makes a good sauce for sherbet or ice cream.

If you're using homegrown grapes, and as many as a quarter of them are unripe (deep red instead of purple), test the cooked, unsweetened juice for pectin to see if you'll need equal quantities of purée and sugar.

> 3 pounds ripe Concord grapes, or a 2-quart
>   basket containing about 3 to 3¼ pounds
> 3 cups sugar

🥄 Place washed, drained grapes in a wide 4-quart saucepan. Crush them with a potato masher to release some juice. Bring to boil quickly, stirring to prevent sticking. Boil about 10 minutes, or until pulp whitens and skins are tender.

Remove from heat and push through a strainer, until you have 4 cups. Use a wooden spoon so that you don't scrape or crack the seeds. At this point, you can let the purée stand as long as 24 hours, if you wish.

When you're ready to make the jam, bring the purée to a boil quickly in a wide 4-quart saucepan, stir in sugar all at once, and continue stirring until it dissolves. Boil rapidly about 20 minutes, or until jell tests almost done. This variety of grape is so rich in pectin that it's easy to overcook. Pour at once into hot, sterilized half-pint or 4-ounce jars or glasses and seal. Makes about 4 cups.

# Tomato-Peach Jam

An unlikely sounding combination—tomatoes and peaches—actually makes a beautiful sweet red jam. My recipe was inspired by an old one that called for yellow tomatoes. Unfortunately, they are largely a backyard fruit today, so I have substituted red tomatoes.

2 pounds firm ripe tomatoes, cored and sliced
2 pounds mature but unripe peaches, pitted
 and cut in chunks
Sugar equal in volume to prepared, cooked
 fruit
2 tablespoons vanilla brandy (page 188) or ½ teaspoon
 vanilla extract

🖎 Place prepared tomatoes and peaches in a wide 4-quart saucepan. Bring quickly to boil, reduce heat, cover, and simmer, stirring occasionally, until fruit is tender—about 15 to 20 minutes. Remove from heat and purée in a food mill or force through a coarse strainer.

Measure; you should have about 6 cups. At this point, if you wish, you may cover the mixture and let it stand overnight.

When you're ready to finish the jam, measure 3 cups of fruit mixture into a wide 2½-quart saucepan and 3 cups of sugar into a bowl. Bring fruit mixture quickly to boil, stirring often to prevent sticking. Stir in sugar all at once and continue stirring until sugar has dissolved and mixture has returned to boil.

Boil rapidly, stirring often, about 40 minutes, or until mixture thickens and ½ teaspoon of it holds its shape when chilled a minute or two on a prechilled saucer in the coldest part of the refrigerator.

When jam tests done, stir in 1 tablespoon of the vanilla brandy or ¼ teaspoon of vanilla extract, and pour or spoon into hot, scalded half-pint or 4-ounce jars or glasses. Seal, and store at least a week before using. Repeat process, using remaining ingredients. Makes 5 to 6 cups.

# Santa Rosa Plum Jam

This jam doesn't hold its lovely rosy color well, so plan to use it young. Store opened jars, between meals, in a cool, dark place, and enjoy the plummy flavor while the jam is fresh — within two months.

2½ pounds firm, slightly underripe Santa Rosa
    variety plums, the paler, the better; cut in
    chunks but reserve pits
½ cup water
2 tablespoons lemon juice, and seeds from the
    lemon
2 cups sugar
1 teaspoon ascorbic acid mixture (see page 29)

❦Place plums and their pits in a wide 2½-quart saucepan with the water. Cover tightly, and place over low heat until juices start to flow and liquid boils. Stir often to prevent sticking.

When plums are very soft — it should take 15 to 20 minutes — put mixture through food mill or coarse sieve to remove pits and purée skins. Add lemon juice and measure. You should have about 4 cups. Return mixture to saucepan and measure depth. Add lemon seeds tied loosely in several thicknesses of dampened cheesecloth or placed in a metal tea ball. Bring rapidly to boil, stirring; boil rapidly about 20 minutes, or until reduced in depth by one quarter. Remove and discard seeds. Add sugar all at once and continue to boil, stirring often, about 20 minutes more, until slightly thick. (The jam will thicken more as it cools.) Stir in ascorbic acid mixture, and pour, boiling hot, into hot, sterilized half-pint or 4-ounce jars or glasses, and seal. Makes about 3 cups.

# Pineapple-Blueberry Jam

Both flavors stand on their own in this rich, dark red jam. (The color surprised me the first time I made the jam; I'd always been told that blue mixed with yellow yields green. Obviously not in the world of fruit.) Pineapple-blueberry jam is great on toasted pound cake, sponge cake, or angel food cake. I sometimes swirl it into softened vanilla ice cream and refreeze it, or layer the jam with vanilla ice cream to make parfaits.

> 2 cups of shredded fresh ripe pineapple (about
>     a 3½-pound fruit)
> 1 pound, or dry pint, ripe blueberries, washed,
>     well drained, sorted, stemmed, and lightly
>     crushed (about 3½ cups before preparing)
> 2¼ cups sugar

❧ Place fruit in a wide 2½-quart saucepan. Bring to boil over medium heat, stirring occasionally. Adjust heat to keep mixture boiling steadily about 10 minutes. Stir occasionally.

Add sugar all at once, and stir until it dissolves and mixture again boils steadily. Adjust heat as necessary to keep jam boiling about 20 minutes, but start testing for set after the first 10 minutes in case the berries have especially high pectin content. Stir often, as this jam tends to stick. It's done when about ½ teaspoon holds its shape in a metal spoon after it rests a couple of minutes on a cool saucer. Spoon at once into hot, scalded half-pint jars, and seal. Makes about 3 cups.

# Peach Jam or Preserves

The peachy flavor and color of this jam (or preserve) are the first of its advantages. Another is that you don't have to use fully ripened fruit, often so difficult to find today. Mature but unripe peaches make a much more flavorful jam. I like it on toast or mixed into plain yogurt or spooned straight from the jar, to satisfy a desire for a little something sweet at the end of a meal.

2 quarts peeled, pitted, thinly sliced peaches
    (about 4 pounds large peaches or up to 6
    pounds small ones)
5⅓ cups sugar
½ cup fresh lemon juice (about 2½ to 3
    medium lemons)
1½ teaspoons ascorbic acid mixture (optional:
    see page 29)
6 tablespoons brandy or sherry (optional)

🍊 Mix prepared peaches with sugar in wide 4-quart saucepan. Heat, stirring, until sugar dissolves completely. For jam, crush fruit with potato masher as it softens. Leave slices whole for preserves. When mixture reaches a full, rolling boil that cannot be stirred down, boil rapidly 10 minutes, stirring occasionally.

Remove from heat and stir in lemon juice and ascorbic acid mixture at once. Pour into a large, deep platter or several shallow, heatproof glass dishes and let stand until cool. (Shallow containers cool quickly, which helps retain jam color.) When cool, cover lightly with waxed paper to protect from dust but permit evaporation. Let stand 24 hours.

The next day, measure the jam; you should have about 8 cups. Place half of it in a wide 2½-quart saucepan, and bring to boil quickly, stirring to prevent sticking. Boil rapidly, continuing to stir often to prevent sticking, about 10 minutes for jam, or until jell test results for preserves. The preserves can take as long as 15 minutes if fruit is very juicy as a result of a rainy growing season.

Remove from heat, stir in half the brandy or sherry, if desired, and skim and stir about 5 minutes to prevent floating fruit if you're making preserves. The stirring is not necessary for jam. Then pour, spoon, or ladle the mixture into hot, sterilized half-pint jars or glasses, and seal. Repeat process with remaining fruit mixture. Makes about 6½ cups.

# Jeanne Jones' Low-Calorie Peach Jam

I'd rather do without than eat most dietetic jams, but this one is different. It tastes as good as it looks and, moreover, it is acceptable for diabetic diets. Mrs. Jones invented it as a variation on strawberry jam for her cookbook for diabetics, *The Calculating Cook*. The flavoring extract is my sole addition.

The jam is delicious as a topping for fresh peaches or fresh blueberries. I sometimes substitute blueberries and orange extract for the peaches and almond extract, to make a spread or sauce for fresh ripe berries.

2 cups peeled, diced, fully ripe fresh peaches
(about 1 pound before preparing)
2 tablespoons water
1 teaspoon unflavored gelatin
1 teaspoon fresh lemon juice
8 drops almond extract
Sugar substitute equal to 2 tablespoons sugar

♦ Place peaches and water in a 1-quart saucepan. Crush fruit slightly with potato masher. Cover tightly and cook 5 minutes over very low heat. Remove cover, mash again quickly, cover, and cook 5 minutes more.

About 1 minute before fruit is done, sprinkle the gelatin on the lemon juice in a small custard cup. It will form a solid mass.

When the 10 minutes are up, remove the saucepan lid, bring fruit and juice quickly to boil, and boil one minute. Remove from heat, add the extract and the gelatin, and stir mixture until no crystals remain. Let cool, uncovered, before adding the sugar substitute. If you add it too soon, heat makes it develop a metallic flavor.

Pour the jam into clean, scalded jars, cover tightly, and refrigerate what you expect to use within a few weeks. For longer storage, leave about ¾ inch of head space, seal, and freeze. But remember that the consistency will not be as good after defrosting. It tends to become watery.

Makes about 2 cups. One cup contains 40 calories, equal to one fruit exchange for diabetic diets.

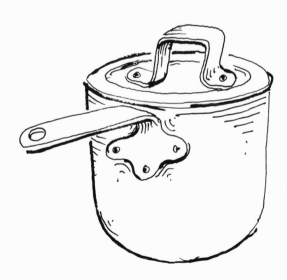

# Jamaica Banana Jam

This jam is one of my West Indian favorites. I adapted it from a booklet published for the University of the West Indies in Jamaica in the 1950s. It is delicious on plain pound cake, and children love it on peanut butter sandwiches. Sometimes I use it instead of custard in tiny tart shells with fresh fruit topping.

¼ cup fresh lime juice (about 1 medium lime)
3½ cups diced firm, ripe bananas (about 6
   medium, or 2¾ pounds)
2¼ cups sugar
½ cup water

🍓 Place lime juice in a 1-quart measure. Peel bananas, and dice directly into lime juice. Stir with wooden spoon after preparing each banana to coat fruit with juice and prevent darkening.

Measure sugar and water into a wide 2½-quart saucepan, and stir to dissolve sugar as you bring syrup to boil. Cover tightly for 1 or 2 minutes, so steam will wash sugar crystals from sides of pan.

Uncover, add banana mixture, and boil over low heat about 30 minutes, or until thick. Stir often to prevent sticking, especially during last 10 minutes.

Jam is done when a spoon scraped across bottom of pan leaves a track that closes slowly, and when jam mounds when stirred.

Spoon at once into hot, sterilized half-pint jars and seal. (Jelly glasses that require paraffin are a poor choice for this jam. It is so thick that it's difficult to smooth the surface enough to allow a secure paraffin seal.) Makes about 4 cups.

# Nectarine Jam

A friend of mine, Grace Manney, uses leftover watermelon pickle syrup in her peach preserves. They taste so good I began experimenting with pickled fruit syrups generally, and found that three kinds of syrup are especially good with nectarines—pickled watermelon rinds (page 127), pickled pears (page 133), and stuffed spiced peaches (page 132).

3 to 3½ pounds mature but unripe nectarines
1 cup water
½ cup syrup from pickled fruit
2⅔ cups sugar

Peel and pit the nectarines, then slice them thinly directly into the water in a bowl of at least 2½-quart capacity. Drain water into a wide 2½-quart saucepan and measure nectarines; you should have 7 to 8 cups. Add to pan, bring quickly to boil and boil steadily until soft —about 20 minutes.

Purée fruit in food mill. Measure. You should have about 3½ cups. Add the syrup and let stand, uncovered, about 12 hours, or overnight. Then stir in sugar and bring to boil quickly in a wide 2½-quart saucepan, stirring to prevent sticking. Boil steadily about 15 minutes, or until jam is thick. It will thicken more as it cools. Pour at once into hot, sterilized half-pint jars or glasses, and seal. Makes about 5 cups.

# Spicy Blueberry Jam

Blueberries have so much natural sweetness that lemon juice, vinegar, or some other acid must be added to make them jell quickly in any recipe without added pectin. Red wine vinegar adds just the right tartness, and the spices make it a much more interesting spread than anything you can buy.

I like this jam particularly on cream cheese or cottage cheese or mixed into plain yogurt. Instead of serving it with plain muffins, I sometimes put a small dollop of jam on each one before the batter goes into the oven.

2 pounds, or dry pints, ripe blueberries,
   washed, well drained, sorted, and stemmed
   (about 7 cups)
½ cup red wine vinegar
3 cups sugar
¼ teaspoon ground nutmeg
¼ teaspoon ground cinnamon
¼ teaspoon ground mace
⅛ teaspoon ground cloves

🍐 Place berries and vinegar in a wide 4-quart saucepan over medium heat. When juice starts to form, increase heat slightly and stir often until mixture boils. Boil steadily about 10 minutes, stirring occasionally to prevent sticking.

Remove from heat, and measure. You should have about 3¾ cups. Add cold water, if necessary, to fill to 4-cup mark. Return mixture to pan.

Measure sugar into a bowl, and stir spices into it.

Bring fruit mixture to boil over medium heat. Add spiced sugar mixture all at once, and stir until jam boils again. Adjust heat so jam boils steadily. Stir often to prevent sticking. The jam should thicken in about 10 to 15 minutes, but start testing for jell after the first 5 minutes, in case the berries' pectin content is exceptionally high. Skim with a slotted spoon as jam cooks.

When jell test results, remove from heat and skim if necessary. A wrinkled skin forms quickly when boiling stops. Spoon into hot, sterilized half-pint jars or glasses or 4-ounce jars, and seal. Store a week or so to mellow. Makes about 5 cups.

# Rhubarb-Strawberry Jam

Surprisingly, the paler the rhubarb, the prettier the deep, rosy color of the jam. The same color rule applies to the strawberries. Both flavors retain their identities in the finished jam, although the rhubarb flavor is the more pronounced. I like this jam best slightly undercooked, to the consistency of a thick sauce rather than a jelly. I sometimes serve the jam (instead of sugar and cream) on fresh strawberries or as a topping for strawberry ice cream.

1 dry pint (about 10 ounces) mature but not
    fully ripe strawberries, hulled and crushed
About 7 cups pale pink rhubarb, trimmed and
    cut in ½-inch dice (about 2¼ pounds
    before trimming leaves and ends)
3 ounces (½ bottle) liquid pectin or about 6
    tablespoons liquefied powdered pectin (page
    44)
About 3 cups plus 6 tablespoons sugar
2 teaspoons ascorbic acid mixture (optional)

❦ Place the prepared strawberries in a wide 2½-quart saucepan and crush them well with a potato masher. Add rhubarb, cover tightly, and cook over medium heat about 10 minutes, or until juice starts to flow from the rhubarb.

Remove cover, raise heat, and continue to boil, stirring often, until mixture is deep pink and rhubarb has fallen apart. This should take about 15 minutes more, or a total of 25 minutes. Remove from heat, and measure. You should have about 4 cups.

Stir in the pectin. Strain and cool 1 teaspoon of the mixture and make pectin test (page 35). Results probably will be broken gel, indicating ¾ cup of sugar per cup of fruit mixture. If results show an unbroken mass of gel, increase the sugar measurement to 1 cup for each cup of fruit.

Stir in the amount of sugar indicated by the test. At this point, you can set the mixture aside (lightly covered) for a couple of days in the refrigerator or a day at room temperature.

When you are ready to finish the jam, measure about 3½ cups of it into a wide 2½-quart saucepan. Bring to boil quickly (stirring often to prevent sticking), and boil rapidly 10 to 12 minutes (continuing to stir often), until jam is consistency of thick sauce. It will thicken more as it cools. If you prefer a firmer jam, cook to jell stage. Remove from heat, stir in 1 teaspoon of the ascorbic acid mixture if you are using it, pour, boiling hot, into hot, scalded half-pint or 4-ounce jars or glasses, and seal. Repeat process, using remaining fruit mixture. Makes about 5 cups and can be served at once.

# Peach Melba Jam

When I first made this recipe, red raspberries cost from $2.50 to $3.18 a pound and peaches only 49 cents a pound, so you can see why it calls for three times as many peaches as raspberries. Surprisingly, the raspberry flavor and color dominate. It's a superb spread for buttered toast, good also on toast spread with cream cheese or Neufchâtel. I prefer the version with seeds, but for people who do not like or cannot eat berry seeds, I've also given directions for a smooth jam.

3 pounds mature but unripe peaches, peeled,
    pitted, and sliced
½ cup lemon juice (reserve seeds)
1 pound ripe red raspberries, rinsed and well
    drained
4 cups sugar
¼ teaspoon almond extract

### METHOD FOR UNSTRAINED JAM

❧Place peaches and ½ cup of water in wide 4-quart saucepan. Place lemon seeds in metal tea ball or tie loosely in a double thickness of dampened cheesecloth. Add seed packet to pan, bring quickly to boil, and boil rapidly 5 minutes, mashing fruit. Add berries all at once, and continue to boil and mash mixture 5 minutes more.

Remove from heat, stir in lemon juice, and pour into a heatproof bowl of at least 2-quart capacity. Let stand, uncovered or lightly covered with a clean cloth, about 24 hours.

The next day, remove and discard lemon seeds, and measure fruit. You should have about 6 cups. Place half of fruit in a wide 2½-quart saucepan and bring to boil over medium heat, stirring often to prevent sticking. When it boils, add 2 cups of sugar all at once and stir until mixture returns to boil and sugar dissolves. Boil rapidly 20 to 25 minutes, or until jam holds its shape when about ½ teaspoon is dropped on a chilled saucer. Stir often during the last 10 minutes to prevent sticking and reduce splattering.

Remove from heat, stir in ⅛ teaspoon of almond extract, and stir and skim for 2 or 3 minutes. Pour or spoon into hot, sterilized half-pint jars or glasses or 4-ounce jars. Seal. Repeat process, using remaining ingredients. Makes about 6 cups.

## METHOD FOR SEEDLESS JAM

❧ Place peaches and ½ cup of water in a wide 4-quart saucepan. Place lemon seeds in metal tea ball or tie loosely in a double thickness of dampened cheesecloth and add to pan. Bring quickly to boil, stirring and mashing to crush fruit. Boil rapidly 10 minutes, continuing to mash fruit. Remove from heat, stir in lemon juice, and pour mixture into a heatproof bowl of at least 2-quart capacity.

Place raspberries and ¼ cup of water in a 1½-quart saucepan and boil, uncovered, about 5 minutes, or until berries are soft. Remove from heat and force through a strainer into the peach mixture. Discard berry seeds. Let jam mixture stand, uncovered, about 24 hours.

The next day, discard lemon seeds and measure fruit. You should have about 5½ cups. Place half of it in a wide 2½-quart saucepan and bring to boil over medium heat, stirring often to prevent sticking. When it boils, add 2 cups of the sugar all at once and stir until mixture returns to boil and sugar has dissolved. Boil rapidly 20 to 25 minutes, or until jam holds its shape when about ½ teaspoon is dropped on a chilled saucer. Remove from heat, stir in ⅛ teaspoon almond extract, and stir and skim for 2 or 3 minutes. It will thicken more as it cools.

Pour at once into hot, sterilized half-pint or 4-ounce jars or glasses. Seal. Repeat with remaining fruit mixture and sugar. Makes 5½ to 6 cups.

# Wine Jellies

Champagne jelly sounds glorious. It is, in fact, a great disappointment. The delicate flavor of champagne, like that of fine still wines, is overwhelmed by the amount of sugar needed in jellymaking. You'd be smarter to drink the champagne and put your preserving money into fortified or flavored wines whose more robust character will withstand dilution by sugar without sacrificing the essential flavor of the wine.

In my experience, the only grape wines that retain any of their true fruit flavor in jelly are those made from native American grapes—Concords, Catawbas, and Niagaras, for instance. If you like these wines, you may like jelly made from them. Pectin manufacturers usually suggest sangría and fortified wines such as port for jellymaking. Frankly, they're not to my taste.

But ginger-flavored currant wine—an English import—makes a superb jelly whose ginger flavor lasts a full year. It's marvelous on toast, or on cream cheese sandwiches. I like it as a glaze for roast pork or ham and as flavoring for poached pears, baked apples, and applesauce.

# Ginger Wine Jelly

2 cups ginger-flavored currant wine
3 cups sugar
3 ounces (½ bottle) liquid pectin

🍋 Place wine and sugar in a wide 2½-quart saucepan, and stir until sugar dissolves. Bring quickly to a full, rolling boil that cannot be stirred down.

Remove from heat, and add pectin all at once, stirring constantly. Skim, if necessary. Pour at once into hot, scalded half-pint or 4-ounce jars or glasses, and seal. Let stand undisturbed until set—it may take 24 hours. Makes about 4½ cups.

# Tarragon Wine Jelly

Tarragon wine jelly, like the ginger wine jelly, is a good relish to serve with or to use as a glaze on roasts. The scent and flavor of tarragon are not as long-lasting as ginger, so plan to use this one soon after the jar is opened. For this jelly I do like a grape wine, Gewürztraminer, because it is naturally spicy and fruity.

The recipe calls for tarragon, but you could just as well substitute basil, rosemary, thyme, chervil, or summer savory.

To make plain wine jelly, omit the herb and the step that produces the herb infusion, and use exactly 2 cups of wine.

Slightly more than 2 cups dry white wine,
    preferably Gewürztraminer
2 tablespoons dried tarragon leaves
3 cups sugar
3 tablespoons fresh lemon juice
3 ounces (½ bottle) liquid pectin
4 or 5 fresh tarragon sprigs (optional)

  Bring 1 cup of the wine to full boil in a small saucepan. Remove from heat, stir in tarragon, cover tightly, and steep 15 minutes.

Strain tarragon "tea" into a 2-cup measure and add enough wine to reach the 2-cup level. Place wine, sugar, and lemon juice in a wide 2½-quart saucepan and bring to boil over medium heat, stirring constantly until sugar has dissolved and mixture reaches full, rolling boil that cannot be stirred down. Boil hard 1 minute, remove from heat, and stir in pectin all at once. Stir and skim, if necessary, for 5 minutes. Place a cleaned, dried tarragon sprig in each hot, scalded half-pint or 4-ounce jar or glass, pour in the jelly, and seal. The fresh herb will rise to the top. Makes about 5½ cups, and it should stand at least a week for flavor to mellow before serving.

# Mint Jelly

Have you ever used mint jelly in chocolate jelly roll or between the layers of a chocolate cake? Ambrosial, that's what it is. So is a parfait of chocolate or vanilla ice cream layered with this mint jelly, melted down with a little water. The jelly recipe is a very old one calling for fresh mint and cider vinegar; I've used white wine vinegar with equal success. But never dried mint: it tends to have a musty smell.

1 large bunch fresh mint (1 cup, packed)
½ cup white wine vinegar or cider vinegar
1 cup water
3½ cups sugar
Green vegetable coloring
3 ounces (½ bottle) liquid pectin

🍓Wash and dry the mint in a salad basket (or roll it lightly in a terrycloth towel and refrigerate for an hour or so). Set aside four 2-inch sprigs from the mint tops.

When virtually no water remains on the mint, measure, and crush to bruise the leaves and release the oil that carries the flavor.

Place crushed mint, vinegar, water, and sugar in a deep 4-quart saucepan, and bring quickly to boil.

While mixture is heating, add enough drops of vegetable coloring to tint jelly as green as you wish.

When mixture boils, add pectin, stirring constantly, and bring to full, rolling boil that cannot be stirred down. Boil 30 seconds and remove from heat at once.

Place a mint sprig in each hot, scalded half-pint or 4-ounce glass or jar. Strain jelly into them. Seal. The mint will rise to the top. Let stand undisturbed until set. Store a week or two for full flavor to develop. Makes about 3½ cups.

# Lemon Rosemary Jelly

This jelly, inspired by a rosemary bush I've nurtured for years, makes a good relish with or a glaze for roast loin of pork, roast fresh ham, or leg of lamb. And it's particularly delicious as a substitute for sugar in the applesauce you might make to serve with these roasts.

The fresh rosemary sprigs do more than dress up the appearance of the jelly. They help retain flavor and aroma, which are apt to fade gradually during storage.

4 medium lemons (about ¾ pound), thinly
    sliced (about 3 cups); reserve seeds
9 cups water
¼ cup dried rosemary leaves, crumbled, or
    about ½ cup fresh ones, bruised
About 5¼ cups sugar
Fresh rosemary sprigs (optional)

Place lemons, including seeds, in the water in a 3½- or 4-quart mixing bowl and let stand, uncovered, overnight, or at least 12 hours.

The next day, transfer mixture to a wide 4-quart saucepan and boil rapidly 30 minutes. Add the rosemary leaves during last 5 minutes of cooking. Remove from heat, cover tightly, and let stand 30 minutes.

Drip mixture through a dampened jelly bag or 4 thicknesses of dampened cheesecloth without squeezing until you have about 5¼ cups of juice. Add an equal amount of sugar, and stir until dissolved.

Place half the juice in a wide 2½-quart saucepan, bring to boil quickly, and continue boiling rapidly 10 to 15 minutes, or until jell tests done. Remove from heat, stir and skim 3 to 5 minutes.

Place a rosemary sprig in each hot, scalded half-pint or 4-ounce jar or glass, pour jelly within ¼ inch of top, and seal. Repeat, using remainder of juice. Makes about 6 cups.

# Rose Geranium Jelly

A rose geranium is one of my favorite house plants, with its spicy fragrance and beautiful blossoms. Our grandmothers used leaves from these plants to perfume and flavor their apple jelly. I like rose geraniums even better in this honey-sweetened spread, because the leaves seem to accentuate the natural spiciness of the honey. I never feel guilty about cutting a few leaves from my rose geranium, because careful pruning is actually good for it.

1 1/2 cups clover honey
1 cup sugar
1 1/4 cups plus 1 tablespoon water
2 tablespoons strained lime juice
7 rose geranium leaves, about 2 inches
    diameter, washed and dried
1/2 bottle (3 ounces) liquid pectin

Mix the honey, sugar, water, lime juice, and 3 of the leaves in a deep 4-quart saucepan.

Bring quickly to a full, rolling boil that cannot be stirred down. *Watch carefully, and remove from heat at once when the foam starts to rise. This jelly boils over very easily.*

Stir in the pectin as boiling subsides. Use a slotted spoon to stir and skim jelly for about 5 minutes, removing leaves as you do so. Place a fresh leaf in each of 4 half-pint jars or glasses, and fill with jelly. The leaves will rise to the top. Seal. Let stand a couple of weeks for flavor to develop.

# Grape Preserves

Pulping uncooked grapes for these preserves is tedious, but worth the time and trouble to me. Because the grapes have an extremely high pectin content even when fully ripe, they are easy to overcook. If the preserves are too stiff after cooling, melt them down with a little water and repack.

2 pounds ripe Concord grapes
½ cup water
2¼ cups sugar

๐Reserving skins, squeeze pulp from grapes. Place pulp in a 1- or 1½-quart saucepan, bring quickly to boil, and boil rapidly about 4 to 5 minutes, or until pulp loses its translucency. Stir occasionally. Force through strainer to remove seeds. Push with a wooden spoon to extract as much pulp as possible.

Place pulp, skins, and water in a wide 1½-quart saucepan, bring quickly to boil, and boil steadily about 15 minutes, until skins are tender. Taste one to be sure.

Remove from heat. At this point you can let the mixture stand, uncovered, as long as 24 hours at room temperature, or you can finish the cooking at once.

Measure fruit. You should have about 3 cups. Add sugar, bring quickly to boil, stirring, and boil rapidly about 10 minutes, or until preserves are almost at jellying stage. Remove from heat, stir and skim if necessary, and spoon into hot, scalded half-pint or 4-ounce jars. Seal. Makes about 3½ cups. I usually let it stand a week before using.

# Strawberry Preserves or Jam

This is my favorite strawberry preserve: not too sweet, not too stiff. If you make it regularly, you'll find no two batches exactly alike, because the pectin content of berries varies widely. Sometimes the jelly will set, with the ruby berries suspended in it like jewels. Other times it will be no thicker than a good dessert sauce—a use for which I heartily recommend it—with coeur à la crème, crêpes, ice cream, even toasted pound cake.

    2 dry pint boxes firm strawberries (preferably a
        third of them underripe)
    3 cups sugar
    3 to 4 tablespoons fresh lemon juice

🍓Gently dump the berries into a large bowl or sink full of cold water. Remove them at once by handfuls to a colander or large strainer to drain well. Pinch off caps, layer berries with sugar in a wide 4-quart saucepan, and let stand about an hour or more, until juice begins to form, if making preserves. For jam, crush the berries with the sugar, using a potato masher.

For either spread, place pan over low heat and stir occasionally and gently until sugar melts. Raise heat and boil rapidly 10 minutes, counting from the time when mixture reaches full, rolling boil. Then, remove from heat and stir in lemon juice at once. Use the larger amount of juice if few of the berries were underripe.

Pour mixture into one or more shallow, heatproof dishes. The quicker it cools, the better its color will be. After it cools, I like to cover the dishes lightly with a clean dishtowel or double thickness of cheesecloth to keep out dust, insects, and passers-by, who may be tempted by the lovely fragrance and color.

About 24 hours later, use a rubber scraper to return all the mixture to the pan. Bring quickly to boil, and boil rapidly 10 to 15 minutes more, timing after the mixture reaches full boil. Unless you have homegrown berries, it probably won't pass the jell test, but will fall in thick drops from a metal spoon held above the steam.

Remove from heat, and stir and skim about 5 minutes to prevent floating fruit. Then pour into hot, scalded half-pint or 4-ounce jars or glasses, and seal. It thickens as it cools. Makes about 3½ cups.

# Half-and-Half Cherry Preserves

Sheer improvisation, this. The natural spiciness of the sour pie cherries makes a splendid foil for the blander, dark sweet variety. The fruit in tender jelly is tart enough to serve as a relish with meat and poultry. But I also like it on cream cheese sandwiches, buttered toast, and cottage cheese.

    1 pound ripe dark sweet cherries, stemmed
        and pitted
    1 pound ripe sour cherries, stemmed and
        pitted
    ½ cup water
    1¼ cups lemon pectin extract (page 40)
    Sugar
    4 drops almond extract

🌣 Place cherries and water in a wide 2½-quart saucepan, bring to boil quickly, and adjust heat to boil rapidly for about 10 minutes, or until dark cherries are tender and juice is blue-red.

Measure. You should have a scant 3 cups. Stir in pectin. Make pectin test: Remove ½ teaspoon of juice, and cool it by holding the measuring spoon on an ice cube. Gently stir the cooled juice into 1 teaspoon of grain or rubbing alcohol in a custard cup. Let stand undisturbed 60 seconds. Pour onto a saucer. If a solid mass of gelatin forms, use 1 cup of sugar for each cup of fruit mixture; if gelatin is in large flakes, use ¾ cup sugar per cup of fruit mixture. *Discard test mixture without tasting.*

Return fruit mixture to saucepan, and measure sugar into a bowl while you bring the fruit mixture to a boil quickly. Add the sugar all at once, and stir until it dissolves and mixture boils again. Adjust heat to retain a steady boil. Stir occasionally while cooking 20 to 30 minutes, or until jell test results.

When it's done, remove from heat, stir in almond extract, and stir and skim, if necessary, for about 10 minutes to cool and prevent floating fruit. Pour into hot, scalded half-pint jars or glasses and seal. Let stand undisturbed until cool and set (about 24 hours). Makes about 4 cups.

# Apple Ginger

Dozens of nineteenth and early twentieth century cookbooks had recipes for this ultrasweet, spicy preserve. It's more confection than spread—something for people with a real sweet tooth. You might try it instead of brown sugar for making candied sweet potatoes.

4 cups sugar
1/2 cup water
1 tablespoon grated lemon peel
3 tablespoons lemon juice
2 pounds firm, ripe, but tart apples, peeled,
    cored, and coarsely chopped (about 5 cups)
1/4 cup (about 2 ounces) coarsely chopped
    crystallized ginger

Place all ingredients in a wide 2 1/2-quart saucepan. Bring to boil, stirring until sugar has dissolved and mixture again boils. Simmer an hour or more, until apples are tender and preserve is thick. Spoon at once into hot, scalded half-pint or 4-ounce jars or glasses and seal. Makes about 4 cups.

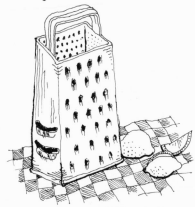

# Preserved Chipped Pears

Like the preceding recipe for apple ginger, this very sweet, spicy preserve was a favorite in the late nineteenth and early twentieth centuries. Some old recipes, called gingered pears or pear ginger, get their flavor largely from Canton ginger. The name apparently came about because the preserved, candied, or crystallized root was imported from the southern Chinese city of Canton.

2¾ cups sugar
1 unpeeled lemon, thinly sliced and seeded
2 pounds (about 4 medium) mature but unripe
    pears, peeled, cored, and sliced about ⅛
    inch thick
⅓ cup, tightly packed, thinly sliced preserved,
    or stem, ginger, drained, or crystallized
    ginger (2 to 3 ounces of either type)

✦Measure sugar into a wide 2½-quart saucepan. Add prepared lemon. Slice pears directly into the sugar and lemon mixture, and stir to coat them. Stir in ginger, and let stand, uncovered, about 24 hours. Stir occasionally. The pears may darken, but this won't show in the finished product.

The next day, bring mixture to boil quickly, stirring. Reduce heat and boil slowly about one hour, or until pears are translucent and mixture is thick and the color of amber. Stir often and watch closely during the last half hour of cooking to prevent sticking and burning. Spoon into hot, sterilized half-pint jars and seal. Store at least 2 weeks before serving. Makes about 3 cups. Flavor and quality hold up well for a year.

# Lime Marmalade

This is one of the easiest, cheapest, and prettiest recipes in my book, particularly if you make it at the peak of the lime season in June–July. It's for real marmalade fans. If you prefer a milder spread, try the honeyed marmalade recipe (page 85).

1½ cups fresh lime juice and about ½ cup
    slivered lime peel (about 6 large limes
    weighing a total of 1½ pounds)
6 cups water
6 cups sugar
Green vegetable coloring
2 tablespoons light rum (optional)

🍓Place the juice in a 2-cup measure. Strip membrane and pulp residue from peel, and reserve. Use a sharp knife or scissors to cut peel into matchstick-size slivers, adding them to the juice until it reaches the 2-cup level.

Place remaining peel and the reserved membrane and pulp in a 1-quart bowl and add 2 cups water.

Place the prepared juice and slivered peel in an 8-quart bowl, and add remaining 4 cups of water.

Let both mixtures stand at least 12 hours, or up to 24. Then place juice and peel mixture in wide 4-quart saucepan, and strain the pulp mixture into it, squeezing to extract as much liquid as possible. Bring quickly to boil, and boil rapidly about 30 minutes, or until peel is tender. Remove from heat. Measure, and add cold water to 6-cup level. Let stand 12 to 24 hours more.

To finish the marmalade, place half the juice-peel mixture in a wide 2½-quart saucepan, bring quickly to boil, add half the sugar all at once, and stir until sugar dissolves and mixture reaches rolling boil. Boil rapidly 25 to 30 minutes, or until jell test results. Remove from heat, tint with a few drops of vegetable coloring, and stir in 1 table-spoon of rum, if desired. (Do not substitute rum extract unless you want the marmalade to taste like an artificially flavored lollipop.)

Skim and stir about 5 minutes to cool the marmalade slightly and prevent floating peel. Pour into hot, scalded half-pint or 4-ounce jars or glasses and seal. Repeat process with remaining ingredients. Store at least 1 week to mellow. Makes about 5 cups.


# Bermuda Marmalade

This pale amber-colored marmalade is both an unusual spread for bread and a versatile cooking ingredient. Melted with orange or grape-fruit juice, it makes a good glaze for baked ham or sautéed ham steak. It is also delicious in baked apples and as a glaze for baked or sautéed bananas. I've named it for Bermuda because it was inspired by a reci-pe in a collection called *What's Cooking in Bermuda* by Betsy Ross (Elizabeth Ross Hunter).

1 small (about ¾ pound) grapefruit
1 medium (about ¼ pound) lime
6 cups water
Sugar

♪Cut the grapefruit, lengthwise, into sixths, and the lime into quarters. Discard the white cores and remove seeds to a small pan of at least 1½ cups' capacity. Cover seeds with 1 cup of the water, and set aside at least 2 to 3 hours.

Strip peel from pulp. Slice pulp a scant ¼ inch thick. Slice peel ⅛ inch thick and 1½ to 2 inches long. Measure. You should have about 2¼ cups, packed, of pulp, juice, and peel. Place the mixture in a 2½- or 3-quart bowl. Cover with remaining 5 cups of water and let stand at least 2 or 3 hours.

Boil seeds 10 minutes to extract pectin while you bring the pulp, juice, peel, and water mixture quickly to boil in a wide 2½-quart saucepan. Strain the seed water into the larger pan, and continue boiling it for a total of about 1 hour, until peel is very tender.

Remove from heat and measure. You should have about 4⅓ cups. Stir in the same amount of sugar until no crystals remain. Measure about 4 cups of the stock back into the saucepan, bring quickly to a boil, stirring occasionally, and boil rapidly 10 to 15 minutes, or until peel is transparent and jell tests done. Stir and skim, if necessary, about 5 minutes to prevent floating peel. Pour into hot, scalded half-pint or 4-ounce glasses or jars, and seal. Repeat process, using remainder of stock. You'll probably need to cook the second batch the shorter time, because there's less stock for it than for the first batch. Store at least one week before using. Makes about 5 cups.

# Amber Marmalade

This is a good example of making lots out of little. I first improvised the recipe to use up two oranges, a lemon, and a lone stalk of rhubarb left over from other recipes. The result was a lovely, amber-colored spread that tastes like mild, sweet orange marmalade. Try it some time on the bottom of the crust you use for apple pie.

    2 medium oranges and 1 medium lemon (total
        weight about 1 pound)
    1 2- to 3-ounce stalk of rhubarb
    Sugar

Thinly slice oranges and lemon, reserving seeds. Tie seeds loosely in two thicknesses of dampened cheesecloth or place in a metal tea ball. Measure fruit; you should have about 2 cups, tightly packed. Place the fruit in a 4-quart mixing bowl. Add three times as much water as you have fruit. Let stand, uncovered, about 24 hours.

The next day, slice rhubarb ¼ inch thick, discarding leaves. Place rhubarb-citrus mixture and bag of seeds in a wide 4-quart saucepan, bring quickly to boil, and boil rapidly 20 to 30 minutes, or until peel is tender and rhubarb has broken up. Stir occasionally.

Remove from heat and let stand uncovered about 24 hours more.

The next day, discard seed bag. Measure fruit mixture. You should have 5½ to 6 cups.

Place 3 cups of mixture in a wide 2½-quart saucepan. Add 3 cups of sugar, stir to dissolve, and bring to boil over medium heat, stirring occasionally. Boil rapidly 15 to 20 minutes, or until jell tests done.

Remove from heat, and skim and stir for about 5 minutes to prevent floating peel. Pour into hot, scalded half-pint jars or glasses and seal at once.

Repeat with remaining fruit mixture and an equal amount of sugar.

Store at least 1 week. Makes about 6 cups.

# Green Tomato Marmalade

I've always been fascinated by old recipes for green tomato marmalade or jam. They sound so good, but I've yet to try one that doesn't caramelize and turn dirty brown by the time it starts to thicken. I finally solved that problem by using whole lemons, which are rich in pectin, instead of just the juice and grated peel. The ginger adds a mildly peppery flavor.

I have also made this marmalade with 2 pounds of green cherry tomatoes, cooked whole. This variety, and a slightly altered cooking method, yields more marmalade, although the flavor is the same. If you use the cherry type, increase water to 1 cup, cook the tomatoes and lemon slices, covered, about 20 minutes in the first step, until the tomatoes and the lemon peel are tender, then proceed as usual. The yield should run closer to 4 or 5 cups.

2 pounds green tomatoes
½ cup, packed, thinly sliced (⅛ inch)
   unpeeled lemon (about 2 medium); reserve
   seeds
1 tablespoon grated crystallized ginger
½ cup water
2½ cups sugar

&#11088;The paler the tomatoes, the better the color of the jam will be. Even those lightly streaked with pink will do. Core tomatoes, and grind coarsely. You should have 4 generous cups. Place prepared tomatoes, lemon slices, ginger, and water in a wide 2½-quart saucepan. Place lemon seeds in a metal tea ball or tie loosely in two thicknesses of dampened cheesecloth and add to pan. Bring to boil quickly. Adjust heat to boil steadily about 15 minutes, until tomatoes and lemon peel are tender. Cool, cover, and let stand about 24 hours.

The next day, measure; you should have about 3¾ cups. Measure sugar into a bowl, and place tomato mixture in the saucepan. Bring to boil quickly, stirring to prevent sticking. Add sugar all at once, and continue stirring until jam boils again. Boil rapidly, stirring often during the last 10 to 15 minutes of cooking to prevent sticking. It should take 30 to 35 minutes for the jam to thicken enough so ¼ teaspoon of it holds its shape after a minute or two on a chilled plate in the coldest part of the refrigerator. Remove from heat while testing. Spoon into hot, sterilized half-pint or 4-ounce jars or glasses, and seal. Let stand 1 week for peel to mellow. Makes about 3 cups.

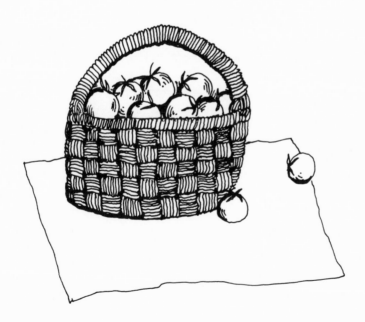

# Tangerine Marmalade

You can make either sweet or bitter marmalade from the ingredients that follow. There are two sets of directions because I find people are about equally divided on the merits of sweet versus bitter. The first set of directions makes sweet (my preference); the second is for those who like traditional Seville orange marmalade.

5 to 6 medium tangerines (about 1½ pounds)
2 medium (3 ounces each) lemons
Sugar

### SWEET MARMALADE

🍓 Score the tangerines in quarters, then peel, reserving all parts of fruit. Remove strings from both peel and segments. Halve segments, reserving seeds, and place in a 4-quart bowl. Slice lemons thinly, reserving seeds, and add lemon slices to bowl. Add the seeds from both fruits, as they're rich in pectin. You should have about 1 quart of fruit and seeds. Cover with 3 cups of cold tap water, and let stand at least 2 hours, uncovered.

Cut enough tangerine peel into shreds or ¼-inch dice to measure 1 cup. Cover with boiling water and let stand until cold. Repeat once, drain well and place in a 1-quart saucepan with 2 cups of water. Boil rapidly 25 to 30 minutes, or until tender. Remove from heat and let stand, uncovered, about 24 hours.

Meanwhile, place the soaked pulp and seed mixture in a wide 4-quart saucepan and boil it 25 to 30 minutes, or until pulp has disintegrated. Remove from heat and let stand, uncovered, about 24 hours. Then drip it through a double thickness of dampened cheesecloth for 3 to 4 hours. Do not squeeze the pulp if you want a fairly clear jelly. (Inevitably, minute particles of pith will separate from the peel, and I never bother trying to filter them out.)

When pulp stops dripping, add the peel and its cooking water to the juice and enough water to measure 4 cups. Stir in 3 cups of sugar until dissolved.

Measure about 3 cups of this stock into a wide 2½-quart saucepan, bring quickly to boil, and boil rapidly about 25 minutes, or until jell test results. Remove from heat, and stir and skim, if necessary, for about 5 minutes to cool marmalade slightly. Then pour into hot, sterilized half-pint glasses or jars or 4-ounce jars. If the peel floats, as it probably will, either stir the marmalade after 15 minutes to distribute it in glasses or shake the sealed jars. Seal glasses with paraffin while hot. Repeat process, using remaining ingredients. Store at least 1 week for peel to mellow and soften. Makes about 3 cups.

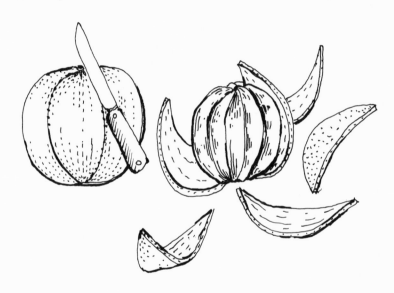

### BITTER MARMALADE

Score the tangerines in quarters, peel, and remove strings from peel and segments. Reserve peel. Halve segments, place in a 4-quart bowl, with lemon slices, and add seeds from both fruits. You should have about 1 quart of fruit. Cover it with 3 cups of cold tap water and let stand at least 2 hours, uncovered.

Shred all the peel finely, and measure. You should have 2 cups. Cover the peel with 3 cups of water, and let it stand 2 hours, uncovered. Then boil the peel 25 to 30 minutes, or until tender.

Boil the pulp-lemon mixture 25 to 30 minutes, or until lemon peel is very tender. Drip through a dampened jelly bag or a double thickness of dampened cheesecloth for 5 to 6 hours into a 2-quart mixing bowl containing the cooked tangerine peel.

Measure. You should have about 4 cups. You can let the mixture stand, covered, overnight or cook it immediately.

When ready to finish the marmalade, stir in 3 cups of sugar until no crystals can be seen, and place half the mixture in a wide 2½-quart saucepan. Bring to boil quickly, and boil rapidly 10 to 15 minutes, or until jell tests done.

Stir and skim, if necessary, about 5 minutes to prevent floating peel. Quickly spoon or pour marmalade into hot, scalded half-pint or 4-ounce jars or glasses, and seal. Repeat, using remaining ingredients. Store at least 1 week for peel to mellow and soften. Makes about 3 cups.

# Honeyed Marmalade

This one is for people who don't really like honey or traditional bitter orange marmalade. It's neither as bitter as the latter nor as flowery in flavor as you expect honey to be. It has a fresh, lively flavor and is the color of the rising sun.

1½ cups finely ground navel orange peel
   (about 3 medium oranges)
1½ cups peeled, finely ground carrots (about
   ½ pound)
6 cups water
Grated peel and juice of about 3 medium lemons
   (2 tablespoons peel and ½ to ¾ cup juice)
2 cups clover honey
2 cups sugar

🥄 Place the prepared orange peel and carrots in a wide 2½-quart saucepan. Add water, stir, and let stand uncovered 12 hours, or overnight.

The next day, bring mixture quickly to boil, reduce heat, and simmer—the surface of the mixture should barely move—for 2 hours. Stir occasionally.

Remove from heat, stir in lemon peel and juice, and let stand uncovered about 24 hours.

Bring to boil again, boil rapidly about 10 minutes, remove from heat, and measure 2 cups of mixture into a wide 2½-quart saucepan. Bring to boil, add 1 cup each of honey and sugar, and stir.

Return to heat, bring quickly to boil and boil rapidly for about 30 minutes, or until thick.

Remove from heat, stir and skim for about 5 minutes, spoon into hot, scalded half-pint or 4-ounce jars, and seal. Repeat process, using 2 cups more of marmalade mixture and remaining honey, and sugar. Store at least a week to mellow. Makes about 5 cups.

# Pineapple Marmalade
# with Kirsch

This pale gold marmalade is for people with a sweet tooth and for everyone who likes the French dessert of pineapple macerated in colorless cherry brandy. Incidentally, the brandy flavor is not too strong for breakfast toast; but my favorite use for this marmalade is on cream cheese sandwiches at teatime.

2¼ cups shredded fresh ripe pineapple (about
    one 4-pound fruit or two smaller ones)
¼ cup strained lemon juice
3¾ cups sugar
½ bottle (3 ounces) liquid pectin
1 or 2 tablespoons kirsch

Peel and core pineapple, and cut fruit into sticks. Cutting with the grain, shred pineapple sticks on the potato slicer slit of a four-sided grater. Stand the grater in a shallow soup bowl as you work. Measure 2¼ cups of the pineapple mixture into a wide, deep 4-quart saucepan. Stir in lemon juice and sugar.

Bring quickly to full, rolling boil that cannot be stirred down. Boil hard 1 minute, stirring constantly. Remove from heat, and immediately stir in the pectin and kirsch. Skim and stir for 8 to 10 minutes to prevent floating fruit. Pour or spoon into hot, scalded half-pint or 4-ounce jars or glasses, and seal at once if using self-sealing lids. If using paraffin, let stand about 30 minutes, until surface firms slightly, before you pour the wax. You may need to stir the marmalade gently if the fruit is floating. Jars with self-sealing lids can be shaken gently after 30 minutes if the fruit is floating. This marmalade sets very slowly and should be allowed to stand undisturbed until it is cold. Store a few days to mellow before serving. Makes 4 to 5 cups.

# Apricot-Pineapple Marmalade

Dozens of contemporary cookbooks include a version of this spread made with canned pineapple and dried apricots. Making it with fresh pineapple takes slightly more time and effort, but I think the fresher, livelier flavor is worth the added work. Cut the apricots with kitchen scissors — it is quicker and easier than using a knife.

1 package (8 ounces) dried apricots, cut in ¼-
   inch strips
Half of a 3 to 3½ pound fresh pineapple
2¼ cups sugar

&#x1F34F; Place apricot strips in a 2-cup measure. Add cold water to the 2-cup level, and let stand, covered, about 12 hours, or overnight.

Peel, core, and remove eyes from pineapple. Grate lengthwise wedges of it on the potato slicer slit of an old-fashioned four-sided grater set in a shallow soup bowl.

When you're ready to cook the marmalade, measure 1 cup of the pineapple and juice — use more pulp than juice — and place it with the apricot mixture in a wide 2½-quart saucepan.

Stir in the sugar, and bring quickly to boil over medium heat, stirring often to dissolve sugar and prevent sticking.

Boil steadily about 15 minutes, being careful to stir often — the mixture sticks easily. When marmalade is thick, spoon it into hot, scalded half-pint jars, and seal. Store it at least 1 week. Makes about 4 cups.

# Lemon Marmalade

This is more than just a spread for bread. It is delicious as a topping for cream cheese cake or spread between the layers of a cake with lemon-flavored frosting. You might try it in bread pudding or steamed pudding, or melt it with a little water to make a sauce for unsweetened fruit or berries. Or substitute it for sugar in baking apples.

2 cups thin, unpeeled, seeded lemon slices,
    cut from about 3 medium or 4 small lemons
    (discard ends)
6 cups water
4½ cups sugar

Place lemon slices and water in a 4-quart saucepan, bring quickly to boil, and boil rapidly about 20 minutes, or until peel is tender and translucent. Drain, reserving pulp and peel, and measure juice. Add enough water to total 6 cups.

Return half the pulp and peel to the saucepan, and add half the liquid and half the sugar. Bring quickly to a boil, stirring until sugar dissolves. Boil rapidly 25 to 35 minutes, or until jell tests done. Remove from heat. Stir and skim, if necessary, about 5 minutes to prevent floating peel, then pour quickly into hot, scalded half-pint or 4-ounce jars or glasses and seal. Repeat process, using remaining ingredients. Store at least a week to let peel soften and mellow. Makes about 4½ to 6 cups, depending on pectin content and ratio of peel to juice. This marmalade tends to weep (liquefy) as it stands because of its high acidity. Either pour off the liquid or stir it back in if you are going to use the marmalade in a sauce.

# Mystery Marmalade

I call this mystery marmalade because few who see and taste it for the first time guess that the primary ingredient is carrots. The natural sweetness of carrots lends itself well to marmalade. And the color is splendid. The recipe is based on one published by the Royal Horticultural Society in London in 1928.

1½ pounds carrots, peeled and coarsely grated
   (about 4 cups)
Juice and finely diced or ground peel of 2
   small lemons
3¼ cups sugar

&#10040;Cook grated carrots in water to cover in a wide 2½-quart saucepan about 15 minutes, or until tender, or steam until tender. Drain well.

Return cooked carrots to the pan. Add lemon juice and peel and sugar. Stir to dissolve sugar. Place over medium heat and continue to stir constantly until sugar has dissolved completely and mixture reaches boil.

Boil steadily about 45 minutes, or until thick, stirring occasionally to prevent sticking.

Ladle into hot, scalded half-pint jars and seal. This is best put up in screw-top jars instead of glasses. The marmalade texture makes a perfect paraffin seal hard to obtain.

Let stand at least 1 week to mellow. Makes about 3½ cups.

# Sally Townson's Tomato Marmalade

It's hard to come up with a tomato marmalade as good as this one, and the bright coral color makes it especially appetizing. I like it with cottage cheese or on cream cheese sandwiches and even as a relish with cold meats.

2¼ pounds firm, ripe tomatoes, peeled, cored,
    and cut in chunks (1 quart, packed)
Pulp and slivered peel of 2 medium (5–6
    ounces each) oranges
Pulp and slivered peel of 1 medium (about 3
    ounces) lemon
4½ cups sugar

🍓Place tomatoes and orange and lemon pulp and peel in a wide 4-quart saucepan. Bring quickly to boil, stirring to prevent sticking. Boil rapidly until peel is tender—15 to 20 minutes. Stir occasionally to prevent sticking.

Measure. You should have about 4½ cups. If not, add cold water to make up the difference.

Return fruit mixture to pan, bring to boil again, and stir in sugar all at once. Continue to heat and stir until sugar has dissolved and mixture again boils.

Boil rapidly, and stir often, about 30 minutes, or until peel is translucent and syrup passes jell test.

Skim, if necessary, and spoon at once into hot, scalded half-pint or 4-ounce jars or glasses. Seal. This marmalade sets very slowly—it may take as long as 48 hours in hot weather to firm up. Store it at least 1 week so peel can soften and flavor mellow. Makes about 5 cups.

# Apricot Butter

A thin layer of this butter spread on unbaked tart or pie shells makes a delicious base for custard or apple fillings. And of course it's good on toast.

11 or 12 ounces (1 box) dried apricots, ground
    finely
1²/₃ cups sugar
2 cups boiling water
¹/₈ teaspoon almond extract or 1 to 2 teaspoons
    brandy or Jasmine Markarian's Apricot
    Cordial (page 179)

🍓 Place ground apricots and sugar in a 1½-quart saucepan, cover with the boiling water, and place over medium heat. Stir constantly to prevent sticking. When mixture boils, reduce heat and cover the pan for 2 or 3 minutes to let steam wash down sugar crystals from the sides of the pan. Remove lid, and simmer and stir for about 5 minutes, until butter holds its shape when a spoonful is dropped onto its surface. Remove from heat, stir in extract or brandy or cordial, and pour at once into hot, scalded half-pint or 4-ounce jars or glasses and seal. Makes about 3½ cups. If you use paraffin, make sure the surface of the butter is smooth before you seal it.

# Pickles, Relishes, and Chutneys

# Dora Thea Hettwer's Schleiss Gurken

This German recipe for sliced pickles is the best of its kind I've ever tasted. They are milder and a little sweeter than my mustard pickles, and I like them particularly with cold cuts, potato salad, and beer.

2½ pounds small, unwaxed cucumbers, sliced
¼ inch thick (about 2 quarts)
1 pound small white onions, peeled and sliced
¼ inch thick (about 2⅔ cups)
6 tablespoons coarse (kosher) salt or 4½
tablespoons uniodized table salt or pickling
salt, dissolved in 6 cups water and cooled
2½ cups small cauliflowerets (about ½ pound)
¼ cup flour
1¾ cups sugar
2½ tablespoons ground mustard
4½ teaspoons celery seed
4½ teaspoons mustard seed
½ teaspoon curry powder
3 cups cider vinegar
½ pound red bell pepper, stemmed, seeded,
and cut in ½-inch chunks (about 1⅓ cups)

☙Place the sliced cucumbers in a 2½- to 3-quart bowl (not aluminum) and the prepared onions in a 1-quart bowl. Divide the cool brine between the two, and weight them with plates and jars filled with water. Let stand 8 to 12 hours.

The next day, cover cauliflowerets with boiling water and boil rapidly about 3 minutes. Drain at once and cover with cold water to stop the cooking. Drain again.

Rinse and drain the cucumbers and onions, and place them with the cauliflowerets in a 4- or 5-quart saucepan.

Mix the flour, sugar, and spices in a 2-quart saucepan, breaking up lumps before stirring in the vinegar slowly. Add diced bell pepper, then bring quickly to boil, stirring constantly. Continue to stir and boil mixture 5 minutes, until the sauce thickens slightly. Remove from heat and keep warm while heating the pickles.

Cover the pickles with boiling water and return to boiling point, stirring often. Drain the vegetables well in a colander, return them to the pan, and add sauce. Stir often as you bring the mixture to a boil over high heat. When it boils, adjust heat to keep pickles hot without cooking them, and quickly pack them in hot, sterilized pint jars, covering with sauce to within 1/4 inch of top. Store at least a month before using. Makes about 10 1/2 cups.

# Mustard Pickles

Crispness, tartness, and a pronounced mustard flavor are what I look for in this type of pickle. The vegetables remain crunchy because they're not cooked, but only heated, first in the soaking water and then in the sauce. On a hot summer's day, I like mustard pickles with cold roast beef, pumpernickel bread, and a glass of cold beer. They're also good with any cold meat or sausages.

1 pound small, unwaxed cucumbers
    (preferably no more than 1-inch diameter),
    cut in 1/2-inch crosswise slices (about 1
    quart)
3/4 pound small white onions (1-inch diameter),
    scalded and peeled
1 pound hard green cherry tomatoes, halved, or
    larger tomatoes, cut in 1-inch chunks
1/2 pound cauliflowerets (about 2 1/2 cups)
1/2 pound bell peppers, stemmed, seeded, and
    cut in 1/4-inch chunks (about 1 1/3 cups)
1/2 cup uniodized table salt or pickling salt or
    1/2 cup plus 3 tablespoons coarse (kosher)
    salt
5 cups water
1/2 cup flour
1 teaspoon ground turmeric
3 tablespoons dry mustard
1 teaspoon celery seed
1 teaspoon mustard seed
1/2 teaspoon each whole cloves and whole
    allspice, tied loosely in a double thickness of
    damp cheesecloth or placed in a metal tea ball
1 cup, packed, light brown sugar
4 cups cider vinegar

&#x2673; Place cucumbers, onions, tomatoes, cauliflowerets, peppers, salt, and water in a 3-quart bowl (not aluminum). Stir well to dissolve salt. Weight the vegetables with a plate and a jar filled with water. Let stand 18 to 24 hours.

The next day, heat the vegetables in the brine in a wide 4-quart saucepan, stirring often, until they are hot to the touch. Drain well in colander.

While the vegetables heat, mix the flour, spices, and sugar in a wide 4-quart saucepan. Gradually stir in the vinegar. Place over medium heat, and stir constantly until mixture is as thick as heavy cream sauce.

Add the hot, well-drained vegetables and continue stirring until they are very hot and sauce is boiling. Adjust heat to keep mixture hot while you quickly pack the pickles in hot, sterilized pint jars. Vegetables should come within ¾ inch of top, and sauce should cover them within ¼ inch of top. Seal. Store at least a month before using. Makes about 5 pints.

# Onie's Bread-and-Butter Pickles

Onie is the family nickname for Aunt Lena Wolf, who was my father's oldest sister and a fine cook. Like most cooks of her time (she was born in 1865), she rarely wrote out precise directions for her recipes. I have her bread-and-butter pickle recipe in her own angular script on a blank page in a dog-eared book, *Good Things to Eat*, published in Topeka, Kansas, in 1921. It calls for one gallon of cucumbers and four large onions, and it makes about eight pints, although she neglected to note this in writing. I halved her recipe for this book. If you want to make the whole thing, either cook it in two batches or use a larger, wider pan.

4 pounds unwaxed cucumbers, 3 to 4 inches
   long, sliced about 1/8 inch thick
1/2 pound onions (2 large ones), peeled and
   sliced 1/8 inch thick
1/2 cup coarse (kosher) salt or 6 tablespoons
   uniodized table salt or pickling salt
Water
2 1/2 cups sugar
1 1/2 teaspoons celery seed
1 1/2 teaspoons mustard seed
1 1/2 teaspoons ground turmeric
2 1/2 cups cider vinegar

Layer prepared cucumbers and onions with salt in a 4-quart bowl (not aluminum). Cover with cold water, and refrigerate, covered, 4 to 5 hours, or overnight.

Drain, rinse, and drain again, then refrigerate in a colander set in the bowl while you prepare the syrup.

Place sugar, spices, and vinegar in a 6- to 8-quart saucepan, stirring to dissolve sugar. When mixture boils, add well-drained vegetables all at once. Stir to encourage even heating, and heat just to the boiling point.

Adjust heat to keep mixture hot but *not* boiling while you use a slotted spoon to fill hot, sterilized pint or half-pint jars within ¾ to 1 inch of top. Cover with boiling syrup almost to overflowing. With a tea strainer, remove spices remaining in pan, divide them among the jars, and seal. (Discard leftover syrup. You may have as much as 2 cups, but it's too watered down by the cucumbers to be reused.) Store at least a month before using. Makes about 8 cups.

*The Pleasures of Preserving and Pickling*

# James Beard's Olive Oil Pickles

I first saw Jim's recipe in his syndicated newspaper column, and it sounded so good I wanted to try it at once. As he wrote, the pickles are crisp and good and different. He serves them with cold meats and fish and even on cream cheese sandwiches. They're also great in cold meat salads. Jim's recipe called for cucumbers and onions by size, but I have measured them by weight, as that is how I buy them at markets and vegetable stands. Otherwise, the recipe is as he described it.

3½ pounds unwaxed cucumbers (3 to 4 inches
    long), sliced no more than ¼ inch thick
1½ pounds onions, peeled and sliced very
    thin
¾ cup coarse (kosher) salt or about ½ cup
    uniodized table salt or pickling salt
1 teaspoon powdered alum
1 quart wine vinegar
½ to ¾ cup olive oil
1⅓ cups, packed, light brown sugar
2 tablespoons celery seed
3 tablespoons mustard seed

❦Mix cucumbers, onions, salt, and alum in a 4-quart bowl (not aluminum) and let stand about 8 to 12 hours, or overnight, in a cool place.

The next day, drain and rinse the vegetables and the bowl. Return the vegetables to the bowl, and add the vinegar. It should cover them. Add more if necessary to do so. Let stand 1 to 4 hours — preferably the latter.

Drain vinegar into a 4-quart saucepan. Add remaining ingredients, and bring to a boil, stirring. Pour boiling hot syrup over the cucumber-onion mixture, pack at once in hot, sterilized pint jars, and seal. Store at least a week before using. Makes about 10 cups.

Don't be alarmed if you have as much as 2 cups of liquid remaining after packing the pickles. The hot syrup draws a lot of water out of the vegetables. The resulting liquid is not flavorful enough to save.

# Spiced Sliced Cucumbers and Onions

Rather like a thick-sliced bread-and-butter pickle, these are only lightly sweetened and not strongly spiced. Great with hamburgers, tuna sandwiches, even cheddar and cheddar-type cheese. It's another of my Canadian favorites, but I prefer the flavor of grated crystallized ginger to the ground ginger in the original recipe.

2 pounds unwaxed, medium-sized cucumbers,
    sliced ½ inch thick
2 pounds small white onions, peeled and
    sliced ½ inch thick
6 tablespoons plus 1 teaspoon coarse (kosher)
    salt or 4 tablespoons plus ¾ teaspoon
    pickling salt or uniodized table salt
2 cups cider vinegar
1½ cups light brown sugar
1 teaspoon cinnamon
1 teaspoon powdered mustard
½ teaspoon ground ginger or 1 tablespoon
    grated crystallized ginger that has been
    rinsed to remove sugar crystals

Place prepared cucumbers and onions in a 4-quart bowl (not aluminum). Mix with 6 tablespoons coarse salt, or 4 tablespoons pickling salt, depending on variety used, and let stand uncovered 12 hours, or overnight.

The next day, drain the vegetables well, rinse in cold water, and drain again. Place them in a large colander set in a mixing bowl, and refrigerate for several hours — at least 3 or 4, but longer won't hurt.

When you're ready to pack the pickles, place remaining salt, vinegar, sugar, and spices in a wide 4-quart saucepan. Bring to boil and boil rapidly for 2 minutes. Add the well-drained, chilled vegetables all at once.

Use two long-handled wooden spoons to turn the vegetables often so they heat evenly. When they are well heated — 10 to 15 minutes — use a slotted spoon to divide them among hot, sterilized wide-mouth pint or half-pint jars. Leave ½ inch of head space.

Bring syrup to full boil, and fill jars to within ¼ inch of top. Work a knife blade around the outer edge between vegetables and jars to release air bubbles before you clean the jar rims with a clean, damp cloth and seal the jars. Cool and store at least 1 month before using. Makes about 5 cups.

# Chunk Pickles

This is a very old recipe. It came from a ninety-one-year-old resident of Connecticut, who got it from her mother. The daughter made the pickles with cucumbers and grapes grown in her own yard. She still lives on the same land, on the shore where the Connecticut River empties into Long Island Sound. Hers are the best sweet pickles I've ever tasted—lightly sweetened, lightly spiced, and crisp. Unlike most pickles, they taste best at room temperature. Chilling overwhelms their delicate flavor.

About 4 pounds unwaxed cucumbers
    (preferably ¾ to 1-inch diameter), cut in ¾-
    inch chunks
¼ cup coarse (kosher) salt or 3 tablespoons
    uniodized table salt or pickling salt
¼ teaspoon powdered alum
1½ cups sugar
1½ cups cider vinegar
1½ cups water
1 teaspoon mixed pickling spice
2 grape leaves for each jar
3 or 4 green grapes (Thompson seedless or
    unripe grapes of other varieties) for each jar
1 small sprig fresh dill per jar

&#9998; Scrub cucumbers in cold water with a vegetable brush before slicing them. Cut out any bruised spots that could spoil the whole lot. Place cucumber chunks in a 4-quart mixing bowl (not aluminum), add salt, and cover with water. Weight them with a plate or plates to keep the chunks from floating. Let stand, covered or uncovered, 16 to 24 hours.

Drain brine into a wide 4-quart saucepan, add alum, heat to boiling, and pour back over cucumbers. Let them stand 12 hours more, again weighted to prevent floating.

When you're ready to pack cucumbers, make a syrup by combining sugar, vinegar, 1½ cups water, and spices in a 2-quart saucepan. Drain the chunks, and discard the brine. Starting with a grape leaf in the bottom of each jar, adding 3 or 4 grapes at random, and ending with a sprig of dill on top, pack the chunks snugly in hot, sterilized wide-mouth pint or 1½-pint jars. As each is packed, set it back in the sterilizer containing several inches of hot water. When all the jars are filled, add hot water to sterilizer if necessary to bring level almost to tops of jars. Cover and heat until cucumber chunks are hot to the touch, but don't allow the water to boil. It might splash over into the open jars.

When chunks are hot, remove one jar at a time from sterilizer, pour off any water that has accumulated (this shouldn't be necessary if you've kept an eye on the kettle to avoid overheating), and fill almost to overflowing with boiling syrup. Top with a grape leaf, clean rim and threads of jar, and seal. Repeat until all are filled. Store at least 2 months before using. (The yield varies, depending on the diameter of the cucumbers. I've gotten 4 pints from 4 pounds of 1½-inch-diameter cucumbers, and 5½ pints from the same weight of ¾- to 1-inch-diameter cucumbers.)

# Parsley Pickles

This is a variation on the preceding recipe for chunk pickles. It is based on an idea I got from reading James Beard's column in which he mentioned two Oregonians who make parsley pickles. Theirs were described as typical sweet pickles made with gherkins, tiny pickling onions, great clumps of parsley, spices, and a sweet-and-sour vinegar bath. So I decided to try my hand at a sliced pickle with similar seasonings.

> 4 pounds small, unwaxed cucumbers
> (preferably about 1-inch diameter or less),
> cut in ½-inch chunks
> ¼ cup coarse (kosher) salt or 3 tablespoons
> uniodized table salt or pickling salt
> ¼ teaspoon powdered alum
> Large bunch of fresh parsley sprigs (preferably
> the flat leaf variety)
> 1½ cups cider vinegar
> 1½ cups water
> 1½ cups sugar
> 2 teaspoons mixed pickling spice with red
> pepper flakes removed

❦ Layer cucumber chunks and salt in a 4-quart bowl (not aluminum). Cover with water, and weight with a plate held in place by a clean, sealed jar of water, to keep the cucumbers immersed. Let stand 16 to 24 hours.

The next day, drain brine into a wide 2½-quart saucepan, add alum, and bring to boil. Pour boiling brine back on the cucumber slices, and weight as before. Let stand about 12 hours.

Drain well. Starting with several large parsley sprigs, pack cucumber slices closely in hot, sterilized wide mouth pint jars, adding more parsley in the middle and on top. I find I can get more cucumber slices in a jar if I pack them on their edges, like wheels. This also makes a prettier pack—nice for gifts.

As each jar is filled, return it to the sterilizer. When they're all packed, add an inch or so of water to sterilizer, and heat, covered, until cucumbers are hot to the touch. It shouldn't be necessary to drain the jars before adding syrup, but if water has accumulated in them, pour it off before proceeding.

While the cucumbers heat, make the syrup in a 1½-quart saucepan. Place vinegar, 1½ cups water, sugar, and spices in pan, and stir over heat until sugar melts. Bring to boil, fill jars almost to overflowing, and seal at once. Store at least 6 weeks before using. Serve at room temperature. Makes about 5 pints.

# Mother's Dill Pickles

As a child, I liked these pickles better than lollipops. The sharp, salty, spicy tang of the pickles was particularly appealing on a typically hot, humid summer day in the South. Even now, I think there's no better accompaniment to a salami or a liverwurst sandwich than a cool, crisp pickle tasting of garlic and dill.

2 fresh grape leaves per quart jar
2 large or 4 small sprigs fresh dill per quart jar
About 3½ pounds small unwaxed cucumbers,
    1 inch or less in diameter and about 3 inches
    long
2 to 4 peeled cloves of garlic per quart jar
1 (1-inch) dried chili pepper per quart jar
    (optional)
1 teaspoon mixed pickling spice per quart jar
Pinch of alum per quart jar
7 cups water
⅓ cup coarse (kosher) salt or ¼ cup pickling
    salt or uniodized table salt
½ cup cider vinegar

Wash and dry grape leaves and dill. Scrub cucumbers under cool, running water and trim away any bad spots. Place garlic, spices, and alum nearby, and place the water, salt, and vinegar in a 2½-quart saucepan to heat while you pack the pickles. Stir the brine occasionally until salt has dissolved.

In each hot, sterilized wide mouth quart jar, pack 1 grape leaf, 1 or 2 sprigs of dill, a vertical layer of cucumbers, 1 or 2 garlic cloves, a second layer of cucumbers, another garlic clove or 2, 1 or 2 dill sprigs, 1 teaspoon of pickling spice (and the hot chili pepper, if desired), a pinch of alum, and another grape leaf.

When all the jars are full, bring the brine to a boil, and pour it, boiling hot, over the cucumbers to fill jars almost to overflowing. Clean rims and threads and seal. Makes about 3 quarts, but the brine is enough for about 4 quarts. Purposely. When the pickles have stopped fermenting, you'll need extra brine to make up for loss during fermenting. If the solids are exposed to air, the pickles will mold and spoil.

## IMPORTANT

Sometimes the lids will seal, forming a vacuum as they should for most pickle products. They should not remain sealed for this type of pickle, which needs air during fermentation. So check the jars after they are cool, and release any lids that have sealed. Store the jars in a shallow pan or dish to catch overflowing brine. When the cucumbers are a uniform olive green color and the bubbling has stopped, remove lids and clean them and the jar threads and rims. Add more brine to cover solids completely and reseal. Chill before serving.

# Sweet Pickled Red Peppers

Just the sight of these vivid scarlet pickles is appetizing, and they taste as good as they look. The bitterness some people object to in raw bell peppers is missing altogether. The sweet pickled rings are delicious on hamburgers and cottage cheese and in a salad, mixed with cold boiled beef or leftover roast beef. You might also try combining drained sweet pickled peppers with sliced tomatoes and raw onion rings to make a salad for cookouts. Incidentally, you can make the recipe with green bell peppers with no change in flavor. But they do fade in cooking, so the pickle isn't as pretty.

> 3 pounds ripe red bell peppers, stemmed, cut
>    into ¼-inch rings, and seeded
> 1 cup coarse (kosher) salt or ¾ cup pickling or
>    uniodized table salt
> 1¾ cups cider vinegar
> 1¾ cups sugar
> 2 tablespoons pickling spice, in a metal tea
>    ball or tied loosely in double thickness of
>    dampened cheesecloth

Prepare pepper rings and soak in salted water to cover about 6 to 8 hours in a 6-quart bowl or saucepan (not aluminum).

Combine vinegar, sugar, spice bag, and ¾ cup plus 2 tablespoons water in a 4-quart saucepan. Bring to boil and boil 10 minutes.

Drain pepper rings, rinse in cold water, and drain again. Add to syrup, bring to boil again, and boil steadily 10 to 12 minutes, or until tender.

With slotted spoon, fill hot, sterilized half-pint or pint jars within ½-inch of top. Boil liquid rapidly until syrupy, fill jars within ¼-inch of top, and seal. Let stand at least a month. Makes about 5 cups.

# Cornichons

True French-style sour pickles should be made from cucumbers a scant half inch in diameter and scarcely two inches long. Unless you grow your own, it's impossible to obtain such small cucumbers in America. But you can make cornichons with somewhat larger ones by allowing extra time for them to cure. I improvised this recipe from the ingredients list on the label of my favorite French brand of cornichons. They are traditional garnishes with French pâtés and terrines and Swiss raclette (the dish of bubbly, molten cheese characteristically served with hot boiled potatoes).

    2 pounds of the smallest unwaxed cucumbers
        available
    2 tablespoons coarse (kosher) salt or 1½
        tablespoons pickling or uniodized table salt
        per quart of water
    For each pint jar to be packed, 1 small white
        onion or shallot, peeled; a pinch of dried,
        crushed red pepper (optional); 1 small clove
        of garlic; ⅛ teaspoon dried leaf tarragon
    1½ to 3 cups cider vinegar or white wine
        vinegar

🌰 Scrub the cucumbers well in cold water with a natural bristle brush, and remove any stems and blossoms. Drain well, and place in a bowl (not aluminum) of at least 2-quart capacity. Dissolve salt in water in the proportions given, and cover cucumbers with the brine. Weight with a plate and water-filled bottle to keep the cucumbers immersed. Let stand at least 12 hours, or overnight.

The next day, drain the cucumbers, dry them without rinsing, and pack, with seasonings and spices, into hot, sterilized wide mouth pint or 1½-pint jars within about ½ to 1 inch of top. Cover almost to overflowing with boiling vinegar, and seal. If cucumbers are tiny, you will need about 1 cup of vinegar per pint jar or ¾ cup per 1½-pint jar. If you have used about a dozen cucumbers 3 to 4 inches long, you'll need about ¾ cup of vinegar per pint jar. If you must work with the large ones, try to get a mixture of straight and curved ones: straight, to pack vertically for the first layer; curved, to pack horizontally in the second layer. Store at least 2 months before using. Makes about 3 pints, using 3- to 4-inch cucumbers.

# Bernice Bixler's Lime Pickles

The lime in these pickles is not fruit, but calcium hydroxide U.S.P., a fine white powder that used to be called slaked lime. Generations of Midwesterners and Southerners have used a solution of slaked lime in water to make pickles so crisp they crackle when you bite into them.

My brother, Mark, who is a chemical engineer, tells me not to worry about the use of calcium hydroxide as a food additive. Because it cannot dissolve completely in water, you'll never get more than a few hundred parts per million in the cold water solution. The second soaking in fresh water removes any powder deposited on the surface of the pickles.

Finding a supply of calcium hydroxide U.S.P. can be the hardest part of the recipe. In urban areas like Manhattan, I have bought it in a few drugstores. Mrs. Bixler, who lives in a small town in Kansas, buys her supply at a lumberyard. For specific sources, see page 201.

You can make Mrs. Bixler's pickles and my green tomato pickles (following recipe) without lime water. The flavor will be the same — sweet and sour, slightly spicy. But the texture will be far less crisp and, I think, not as delicious.

3½ pounds unwaxed cucumbers, preferably no
　　more than 1¼ to 1½ inches in diameter,
　　sliced about ⅛ inch thick
¼ ounce (1 bottle) calcium hydroxide U.S.P.
　　(formerly slaked lime), dissolved as label
　　directs in 1 gallon cool water
5 cups cider vinegar
2¾ cups sugar
2 teaspoons coarse (kosher) salt or 1½
　　teaspoons uniodized table salt or pickling
　　salt
½ teaspoon whole cloves
½ teaspoon celery seed
1 teaspoon mixed pickling spice

❧Place prepared cucumbers in the lime water solution in a pan
or bowl of at least 8-quart capacity (not aluminum), and let stand
about 24 hours. The next day, use a skimmer or a slotted spoon to
remove the cucumber slices to a 4-quart bowl (not aluminum). Rinse
them well in cool water, and drain well, repeating the process a second time. Cover with cool tap water and let stand about 3 hours.

While cucumbers are soaking, place vinegar, sugar, salt, and
spices in a 2-quart saucepan, bring to boil, and stir until sugar dissolves. Remove from heat and let cool.

Drain the cucumber slices well, return them to bowl, cover with
syrup, and let stand 12 hours or overnight.

The next day, place cucumbers and syrup in a wide 6- or 8-quart
saucepan, bring to boil, stirring occasionally, and boil 35 minutes, or
until slices look clear.

Use a slotted spoon to divide cucumber slices among hot, sterilized pint and/or 1½-pint jars within ½ inch of top. Bring syrup to
boil, fill jars almost to overflowing and seal. Let stand at least 1 week
before using, but a month is even better. Makes about 5½ pints.

# Green Tomato Pickles

Like the preceding recipe for Bernice Bixler's lime pickles, these are kept especially crisp by presoaking in a solution of calcium hydroxide U.S.P., a fine white powder whose other uses include an old-fashioned remedy for colicky babies. Pickles made without the calcium hydroxide are just as flavorful, but less crisp.

If as much as ½ cup of syrup is left over, cook a few carrot sticks in it in a covered saucepan until they are tender but still crisp. Chill and serve as icebox pickles or snacks.

1 tablespoon (½ bottle) calcium hydroxide
   U.S.P. (formerly slaked lime; source, page
   201), dissolved as label directs but in only 2
   quarts of cool water
3 pounds hard green plum tomatoes, sliced a
   scant ¼ inch thick (about 9 cups)
½ pound small white onions, peeled and
   sliced about ¼ inch thick (about 1⅓ cups)
1½ cups sugar
3 cups cider vinegar
1 teaspoon peppercorns
¼ teaspoon whole cloves
1 teaspoon whole allspice
2½ inches broken stick cinnamon
¼ teaspoon each of mustard seed, celery seed,
   and grated crystallized ginger per pint of
   pickles


Place calcium hydroxide and water in a 4-quart bowl (not aluminum), and stir often for 1 hour.

Add sliced tomatoes and onions, and let stand about 24 hours. Stir occasionally.

The next day, drain and rinse the vegetables, drain again, and soak them in cold water to cover for 2 to 3 hours.

Drain the vegetables in a colander while you prepare the syrup. Mix the sugar and vinegar in a wide 4-quart saucepan. Tie the peppercorns, cloves, allspice, and cinnamon in a dampened cheesecloth square 3 or 4 layers thick or place them in a metal tea ball. Add the spice bag to the pan, bring quickly to a boil, and boil rapidly 5 minutes. Add the vegetables all at once, and cook about 15 minutes, stirring occasionally, and timing from the point at which the syrup returns to a boil. Spoon, boiling hot, into hot, sterilized pint jars. Add mustard and celery seeds and crystallized ginger, and make sure the solids are covered by about 1/2 inch of syrup. They'll expand as they cool. Store 4 to 6 weeks before using. Makes about 4 pints.

# Blanche Rottluff's Pickled Green Cherry Tomatoes

This is a flexible recipe for which only approximate measurements can be given for some ingredients. And the yield depends, of course, on the size of the tomatoes you can obtain; it will vary greatly. These pickles are milder than dilled tomatoes I make with my mother's pickle brine. They make an unusual cocktail snack, served plain or with a dip or skewered on toothpicks with squares of sharp cheddar.

> About 1 pound green cherry tomatoes, each
>     pierced two or three times with a small skewer
> 1 small clove garlic per half-pint jar
> 3 whole black peppercorns per half-pint jar
> ¼ cup coarse (kosher) salt or 3 tablespoons
>     pickling or uniodized table salt
> 2 cups water
> 1 cup cider vinegar

Pack prepared tomatoes in hot, sterilized half-pint or pint jars within 1 inch of top. Add garlic and peppercorns. Dissolve the salt in the water and vinegar, and fill jars almost to overflowing with this brine. You can use the brine hot or cold; the pickling will be completed faster with hot brine. If you use cold brine, check the jars when fermentation stops (usually in 3 to 4 weeks), and add more brine if necessary to cover the tomatoes and prevent spoilage. Let stand at least 1 month if packed with hot brine or 6 weeks if cold brine was used. Makes about 4 half-pints using tomatoes ranging in size from ½ inch to 1¼ inches diameter, with about half small and half large ones.

To make enough brine for 6 to 7 wide mouth pint jars, I use 4 cups water, 2 cups cider vinegar, and ½ cup pickling or uniodized table salt or ¾ cup coarse (kosher) salt. It's almost impossible to estimate the poundage of tomatoes needed for this size batch. I've made it only when I could work out of a friend's garden, to salvage the last of the tomatoes before they were killed by frost.

# India Relish

This differs from most nineteenth-century India relish recipes in that it contains olive oil and curry powder as well as other traditional curry spices. Because it's heated rather than cooked, it remains crisper than other relishes and is especially good with hamburgers and cold meats of all sorts, including sausages.

1 cup stemmed, seeded, chopped green
    peppers (about 1 pound)
4 cups chopped cabbage (about 1 pound)
2 cups chopped onions (about 1 pound)
1¼ cups chopped unwaxed cucumbers (about
    ½ pound)
½ cup chopped red bell peppers (about ½
    pound)
3 tablespoons uniodized table salt or pickling
    salt or ¼ cup coarse (kosher) salt
1⅓ cups, packed, light brown sugar
4 teaspoons mustard seed
1 tablespoon celery seed
⅛ teaspoon ground turmeric
¼ teaspoon ground black pepper
3 cups cider vinegar
5 tablespoons ground mustard
½ teaspoon curry powder
¼ cup olive oil

&#x2642; Mix prepared vegetables and salt in a bowl (not aluminum) of at least 2½-quart capacity.

Mix sugar with mustard and celery seeds, turmeric, and black pepper in a wide 4-quart saucepan. Stir in 2½ cups of the vinegar, and bring to boil quickly. Boil steadily for 5 minutes, then pour mixture over the vegetables and let stand, uncovered, until cool.

Mix ground mustard and curry powder in a 1-cup measure, and stir in the remaining ½ cup vinegar slowly until no lumps remain. Stir in olive oil, and set aside.

Drain syrup back into the saucepan, bring to boil quickly, and add the vegetables all at once. Heat and stir just until vegetables are thoroughly hot. Do not let the mixture boil. Stir in the spiced vinegar and oil mixture and pack at once in hot, sterilized half-pint or pint jars and seal. Store at least 6 weeks before using. Makes about 8 cups.

# Piccalilli

When I was growing up in Arkansas, piccalilli was a relish we ate with cold cuts and hamburgers. Years later, a friend from New England told me it is traditional with baked beans in her part of the country. It probably reached our coast via Old England, whose sea captains and army officers would have developed a taste for this highly seasoned chopped vegetable pickle in India. Some old American recipes even call it Indian pickle.

1¼ pounds green tomatoes, coarsely ground
   (3 to 3½ cups)
¼ pound bell peppers, preferably half red and
   half green, stemmed, seeded, and coarsely
   ground (about ½ cup measured with the hot
   pepper following)
1 hot pepper, about 5 to 6 inches long,
   stemmed, seeded, and coarsely ground
½ pound onions, peeled and coarsely ground
   (about 1 cup)
¾ pound cabbage, coarsely ground (about ¾
   cup)
1 tablespoon mustard seed
1 tablespoon celery seed
1 tablespoon coarse (kosher) salt or 2
   teaspoons uniodized table salt or pickling
   salt
2 cups cider vinegar
1¼ cups sugar

⚬ Combine all ingredients in a wide 4-quart saucepan. Bring to boil quickly, stirring occasionally. Boil slowly about 30 minutes, or until mixture thickens slightly. Spoon, boiling hot, into hot, sterilized half-pint or pint jars and seal. Store at least 1 month. Makes about 7 cups.

# Helene Robinson's Pepper Hash

For hamburgers, this old-fashioned relish is hard to beat. I also like it mixed with cottage cheese. The recipe came to me from my Kansas cousin, Patricia Sears, who got it from a friend in Wichita in 1927.

1½ pounds (about 6 medium) green bell
    peppers, stemmed, seeded, and coarsely
    ground (about 3 cups)
1½ pounds (about 6 medium) red bell peppers,
    stemmed, seeded, and coarsely ground (about 3
    cups)
1½ pounds (about 6 medium) yellow onions,
    peeled and coarsely ground (about 3 cups)
1½ cups sugar
1 cup cider vinegar
2¼ teaspoons coarse (kosher) salt or 1½
    teaspoons pickling salt or uniodized table
    salt

Drain prepared peppers and onions in a colander lined with a double thickness of cheesecloth. Transfer the vegetables to a heatproof bowl, cover with boiling water, and let stand 5 minutes.

Drain again, and place vegetables in a wide 2½-quart saucepan. Stir in sugar, vinegar, and salt. Bring to boil quickly, reduce heat, and boil steadily 20 to 30 minutes, or until vegetables are cooked but not mushy. Ladle or spoon at once into hot, sterilized half-pint jars, and seal. Store at least a month. Makes about 6 cups.

# Demetria Taylor's Corn Relish

I've made corn relish with and without cabbage. With is better, although, oddly enough, the finished product doesn't have the characteristic flavor of cabbage. This recipe is a scaled-down version of an old New England one. It is good with roasts, broiled or boiled meat, fried chicken, and, of course, hamburgers.

4 cups, packed, fresh corn (kernels from about
   8 medium ears)
1/4 pound onions, peeled and coarsely chopped
   (about 1/2 cup)
1/2 pound bell peppers, stemmed, seeded, and
   coarsely chopped (about 1 cup); if possible,
   buy half red and half green ones
1 cup (about 1/4 pound) finely chopped
   cabbage
2 tablespoons coarse (kosher) salt or 1 1/2
   tablespoons pickling or table salt
1/4 teaspoon ground white pepper
1 1/2 tablespoons ground mustard
1/2 teaspoon mustard seed
1 cup sugar
2 cups cider vinegar

Place all ingredients in a wide 4-quart saucepan, and bring to boil over medium heat, stirring occasionally. Simmer 1 hour. Keep over low heat as you quickly spoon the relish into hot, sterilized half-pint jars. Seal. Store at least a month before serving. Makes about 5 cups.

# Bess Dewing's
# Sweet/Hot Pickle Relish

The real difference between this and other piccalilli-type relishes is the spiciness that comes from fresh hot chili peppers. I like it with cold cuts, or mixed with cottage cheese on a salad plate, or stirred into mayonnaise to serve with cold fish steaks or fillets.

2½ pounds unwaxed cucumbers, coarsely
    ground (about 5½ cups)
¾ pound bell peppers, preferably half red and
    half green, stemmed, seeded, and coarsely
    ground (about 1 cup, measured with hot
    peppers following)
2 hot peppers, each about 5 to 6 inches long,
    stemmed, seeded, and coarsely ground
¾ pound onions, peeled and coarsely ground
    (1½ cups)
3 tablespoons coarse (kosher) salt or 2
    tablespoons uniodized table salt or pickling
    salt
3 cups cider vinegar
1¼ cups sugar
1½ teaspoons mustard seed
¾ teaspoon ground turmeric
1 tablespoon whole cloves
1 tablespoon broken stick cinnamon
1½ teaspoons whole allspice
¾ teaspoon cracked nutmeg*

*This is a good way of using end pieces of nutmeg from a grinder. Wrap one or two loosely in a corner of a clean dish towel and whack them sharply with a hammer. Measure the amount you need; reserve any leftover chunks to flavor milk for custard or rice pudding.

◌ Mix prepared cucumbers, bell and hot peppers, onions, and salt in a 3-quart bowl (not aluminum), and weight with a plate to keep vegetables from floating. Let stand at least 12 hours, or overnight.

The next day, drain, rinse, and drain well. Place in a wide 4-quart saucepan with the vinegar, sugar, mustard seed, and turmeric. Place the cloves, cinnamon, allspice, and nutmeg in a metal tea ball, or tie loosely in 3 or 4 thicknesses of dampened cheesecloth. Add the spice mixture to pan, and bring to boil quickly, stirring occasionally. Reduce heat and simmer 1 hour, stirring occasionally.

Discard spice bag, and pack relish, boiling hot, into hot, sterilized half-pint jars. Store at least 1 month before serving. Makes about 7½ cups, but you may get 8½ if the peppers are especially meaty.

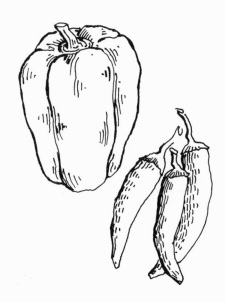

# Beet Relish

This deep red relish has a crisp texture that's good with hamburgers and meat loaf or as an ingredient in meat loaf. And it's delicious with pot roast or boiled beef. Mixed with mayonnaise or sour cream, it makes a beautiful pink and tangy salad dressing.

1/2 pound green bell peppers, stemmed, seeded, and
    coarsely ground (about 3/4 cup pulp and
    juice)
2 cups coarsely ground, cooked beets (about 1
    pound raw, weighed without tops)
1/2 pound onions, peeled and coarsely ground
    (1 cup)
1 1/4 pounds cabbage, coarsely ground (3 1/4
    cups, lightly packed)
1 cup sugar
1 teaspoon uniodized table salt
1 cup cider vinegar
1 tablespoon dehydrated horseradish or 2
    tablespoons prepared horseradish, drained

  Place all the ingredients except the horseradish in a 4-quart saucepan and bring to boil over medium heat, stirring often. Boil steadily about 30 minutes, stirring occasionally, until mixture is thick. Add horseradish during the last five minutes of cooking time.

Spoon at once into hot, sterilized half-pint or pint jars within 1/4 inch of top. Run a scalded knife blade around side of jar to release air bubbles, and seal. Store at least a month before serving. Makes about 7 cups.

# Sweet Cucumber Relish

Great with all sorts of cold meats and poultry, this relish is from a pamphlet published in Canada during the Depression. Except for more complete cooking directions, I made no changes in the original.

2½ pounds unwaxed cucumbers, coarsely
   ground (about 4½ cups)
¾ pound (3 medium) onions, peeled and
   coarsely ground (about 1½ cups)
3 tablespoons coarse (kosher) salt or 2
   tablespoons uniodized table salt or pickling
   salt
¼ cup drained, rinsed, and finely chopped
   preserved ginger
1 cup cider vinegar
½ cup, packed, light brown sugar
½ teaspoon ground cinnamon
½ teaspoon ground mustard
Salt if needed

Mix ground cucumbers and onions with salt in a 2-quart bowl (not aluminum), and let stand, uncovered, about 12 hours, or overnight. Drain well and place in saucepan with remaining ingredients. Taste for saltiness, and add ½ teaspoon or more if desired.

Bring quickly to boil, and boil rapidly 10 minutes, stirring occasionally.

Spoon at once into hot, sterilized half-pint or pint jars, and seal. Store at least 4 weeks. Makes about 5 cups.

# Spiced Cherries

Although spiced cherries set like jelly, they're more of a relish than a spread. Sometimes I add blanched halved or slivered almonds during the last 5 minutes of cooking to make a conserve. Either way, they're good with pork or turkey.

2 pounds ripe dark sweet cherries
3 cups sugar
¾ cup red wine vinegar
½ teaspoon ground mace
½ teaspoon ground cinnamon
⅛ teaspoon ground cloves
¼ to ½ cup blanched almond halves or slivers
   (optional)

❧ Stem and pit the fruit, preferably with a plunger-type pitter that leaves the cherries whole.

Combine remaining ingredients in a wide 4-quart saucepan; bring quickly to boil, stirring to dissolve sugar. When the syrup boils, add the cherries all at once. Boil steadily, stirring occasionally, about 40 minutes, or until a teaspoon of syrup thickens in 2 to 3 minutes on a prechilled saucer in the coolest part of the refrigerator.

Pour while hot into hot, sterilized half-pint jars, and seal. Store at least 1 month. Makes about 4½ cups without almonds, about 5 cups with them.

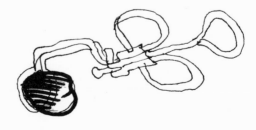

# Peppery Pear Relish

The Chinese, who invented chow-chow as a mustard-flavored mixed vegetable pickle, might be surprised at this Texas version. The main ingredient is fruit, and it is particularly good with ham, pork, hamburgers, and cold cuts. I came across it in Alma Lee Holman's Cookbook column in the Taylor (Texas) *Press*. The version she printed called for 25 pears and 12 hot peppers. I've reduced both the size of the recipe and the potency, leaving some leeway in the number of peppers to use.

2¼ to 2½ pounds semiripe pears (pale green
    tinged with yellow), peeled, cored, and
    coarsely ground (about 4 cups)
1 pound (3 medium) onions, peeled and
    coarsely ground (about 2 cups)
3 to 6 bottled or pickled red hot peppers,
    drained and coarsely ground
1½ teaspoons coarse (kosher) salt or 1
    teaspoon table salt or pickling salt
½ cup prepared yellow mustard
¾ cup cider vinegar
¾ cup sugar
1 teaspoon celery seed
1 teaspoon ground coriander

Mix all the ingredients in a wide 2½-quart saucepan, bring to boil over medium heat, stirring occasionally, and adjust heat to boil steadily about 45 minutes, or until thick. Stir occasionally.

Spoon, boiling hot, into hot, sterilized half-pint or pint jars, and seal. Store at least 4 weeks. Makes about 7 cups.

# Nika Hazelton's Sweet-Sour Plum Relish (Saure Pflumli)

Most pickled plums are too sharp for my taste, so I was delighted to find this recipe in Nika's *The Swiss Cookbook*. It is, as she wrote, an old-fashioned relish for any kind of roast or boiled meat and fowl, and for cold cuts. I have expanded her directions slightly but otherwise made no changes.

For a spicier relish, I sometimes substitute ginger-flavored currant wine for the dry red wine.

2⅓ cups sugar
1½ cups dry red wine
1½ cups red wine vinegar
15 whole cloves
4 inches stick cinnamon, broken
3 pounds firm, ripe, purple Italian (prune) plums

Place sugar, wine, and vinegar in a 2-quart saucepan. Tie spices loosely in two thicknesses of dampened cheesecloth or place in a metal tea ball. Add spice bag to syrup, bring to boil, and simmer, covered, 5 minutes. Cool.

While syrup cools, wash and dry plums, prick them three times each with a small skewer, and place them in a 3-quart bowl. Cover with cooled syrup, and let stand about 8 hours, or overnight. The syrup will not cover the fruit completely at first, but do not add more.

The next day, drain syrup, bring to boil, and let cool again before pouring it back over fruit. Let stand another 8 hours. Then place plums and syrup in a wide 4-quart saucepan and cook over lowest possible heat until the skins begin to tear in one or two places and plums are hot. If the syrup boils or the plums cook too long, the skins will shrivel and the fruit will shrink.

Use a slotted spoon to divide plums among 4 hot, sterilized wide mouth pint jars, and drape a clean towel over them to protect the fruit while you quickly boil down the syrup to the consistency of heavy cream. Nika cools the syrup before pouring it over the plums and sealing the jars; I usually fill them while hot and seal at once. Let stand 2 or 3 weeks to mellow. Makes about 8 cups.

# Pickled Watermelon Rind

This is a flexible recipe, easy to adjust at any point in terms of flavoring and proportion of syrup to solids.

Watermelons today have thinner rinds than those of a generation or more ago, so the old recipes that call for 1-inch cubes just don't work. You're lucky to get ½-inch cubes. And they're easier to pack than large cubes because you can get more into a jar, especially a half-pint one.

Buy 2½ to 3 times the weight in melon that you want in unpeeled rind. Cut or scoop out the red meat and save it for other purposes. Use a large, very sharp knife to cut the rind into strips about 3 inches wide and then into ½-inch strips. I find a knife with serrated edge is best for this step, and a grapefruit knife is best for removing any vestiges of pink meat and the hard, dark green outer rind. Cube the prepared strips, and measure them.

Cover every 4 cups of cubes with a brine of 3 tablespoons un-iodized table salt or pickling salt dissolved in 1½ quarts of water. If necessary to cover rind completely, add more brine made in the proportions of 1 tablespoon salt to each 2 cups of water. Weight with a plate and a jar of water to keep rind from floating. Let it stand about 24 hours at room temperature in cool weather, or in the refrigerator if it's hot.

The next day, drain the rind, rinse it in cold water, and drain again. Tip the rind into a large saucepan, cover with boiling water and cook 8 to 10 minutes, timing from the point at which water reboils. When the rind is easy to pierce with a toothpick, drain it well, measure, and cover with this boiling syrup for each 8 cups of uncooked rind:

> 4 cups sugar
> 2 cups white vinegar or white wine
>     vinegar
> 1/8 teaspoon oil of cloves or 1 teaspoon whole
>     cloves
> 1/8 teaspoon oil of cinnamon or 4 inches stick
>     cinnamon, broken

🍂 I find spice oils give a better flavor without discoloring the pickles. They are more expensive than whole spices and often hard to find, but they can be ordered by mail (for sources, see page 201). If you prefer whole spices tie them loosely in four layers of cheesecloth or place them in a metal tea ball.

Boil the sugar, vinegar, and spice oils or whole spices in a 1- or 1½-quart saucepan for 5 minutes, then pour syrup on cooked rind. If the syrup does not cover fully, boil a bit more, using 2 parts sugar to 1 part vinegar, but do not use more spices at this point.

Weight the rind to keep it submerged, and let stand, uncovered, about 24 hours.

The next day, taste a cube of rind. If it's too mild, drain the syrup into a 1- or 1½-quart saucepan and add more solid spices to the bag or tea ball or a few more drops of spice oils. Bring to boil again, and pour back over rind. Weight it as before, and let stand another 24 hours.

On the third day, place fruit and syrup in saucepan, bring to boil, and, when cubes are thoroughly hot, use a slotted spoon to pack them loosely into hot, sterilized half-pint jars within ½ inch of top. When all jars have been filled, bring syrup to boil, fill jars within ¼ inch of top, and seal. The solids will expand as they cool. Store a week or so to mellow. Serve well chilled. You should get about 5 cups of pickled rind from every 2 pounds of rind, weighed after parboiling but before soaking in syrup.

For a fancier pack, I like to cut the rind in circles, but there's a lot of waste to this method and the quantity per jar is less.

# Stuffed Spiced Peaches

If you like pickled peaches, try these stuffed, spiced ones for a change. They are filled with ginger instead of studded with cloves. Cinnamon splints both hold the halves together and give them flavor. As a garnish for plain roast duck, they're hard to beat.

If you double or triple the recipe, cook only one batch at a time. The peeled, unpitted peaches can stand safely in the acidulated water, but they tend to darken if left to drain too long. If you can get ascorbic acid mixture, use 2 teaspoons of it instead of the salt and vinegar in the soaking water for better control of darkening, and add 2 teaspoons of the mixture to each jar before sealing it.

    1 or 2 sticks of cinnamon
    Crystallized or drained, preserved ginger
    2 cups sugar
    1 cup white vinegar
    1 tablespoon each of salt and vinegar dissolved
        in 1 quart of cold water
    2 pounds semiripe, small, freestone peaches

♨Break the cinnamon into narrow splints and finely grate enough ginger to provide ⅛ to ¼ teaspoonful for each peach.

Place sugar and the cup of vinegar in a 1½-quart saucepan, and stir to dissolve sugar.

Mix salt and the tablespoon of vinegar in water in a 4-quart bowl (not aluminum). Scald and peel peaches, dropping each one as peeled into the acidulated, salted water to prevent darkening.

When all the peaches are peeled, halve and pit them one at a time, place ginger in the cavities, put cut sides together and fasten each peach with 1 or 2 cinnamon splints at each end. Place the stuffed peaches on several thicknesses of paper toweling to drain. Bring sugar and vinegar to boil, and boil rapidly 5 minutes. Place peaches in a bowl, cover with boiling hot syrup, and weight with a plate and a jar filled with water. Let stand about 24 hours.

The next day, use a slotted spoon to remove the peaches to a large colander or rack placed over a pan to catch drippings. Pour the syrup into a wide 2½-quart saucepan, and boil up again. Return peaches to bowl, and cover with boiling syrup and weight as before.

The third day, drain peaches as before, place syrup in a saucepan, and boil it rapidly until thick. Then heat peaches, a single layer at a time, turning to heat evenly and transferring them when hot to a hot, sterilized wide mouth quart jar. Cover almost to overflowing with boiling hot syrup, and seal. Store at least 6 weeks before using. Makes about 1 quart.

# Sweet Pear Pickles

Seckel pears vary so widely in size and shape that the yield from this recipe is difficult to predict. Inevitably, I have leftover syrup, so I bottle it and use it to baste ham or pork roasts, or to thin mayonnaise for fruit salad. The white vinegar makes a pale, pretty syrup that helps the pears keep their natural color.

Spiced fruit traditionally is served as a relish with roasts and poultry, but I find these pears a pleasantly piquant dessert when served with a spoonful or two of their syrup or a scoop of vanilla ice cream.

1 tablespoon salt
3 cups plus 1 tablespoon vinegar
2½ pounds firm, ripe seckel pears
¾ teaspoon whole cloves
¾ teaspoon whole allspice
¾ teaspoon broken stick cinnamon
1 tablespoon dried cracked ginger or 1 inch of
    dried stem ginger
3 cups sugar

🍐 Place 2 quarts water, salt, and 1 tablespoon vinegar in a 4-quart mixing bowl (not aluminum). Peel pears, removing blossom end but leaving stem on. Drop each pear as it is prepared into the water to prevent darkening.

Tie the spices loosely in a double thickness of dampened cheesecloth or place them in a metal tea ball, and place in a wide 2½-quart saucepan with remaining ingredients and 2 cups of water. Stir to dissolve sugar, bring to boil over medium heat, and boil rapidly 10 minutes.

Drain pears. Rinse in cold water, and drain well.

Add to boiling syrup only as many pears at one time as will fill one jar. Cook them about 10 minutes, or until a toothpick pierces pears easily. As you remove each pear let it drain well through a slotted spoon before placing in hot, sterilized wide mouth pint, 1½-pint, or quart jars. Cover packed jars with a clean dish towel to keep them warm while you cook and pack remaining pears.

Boil syrup rapidly for 10 minutes. Discard spice bag. Pour syrup at once over pears, covering them completely and leaving about ¼-inch of head space in jars. Seal at once.

Store at least 1 month in cool, dark, dry place before serving.

Using pears about 2 inches in diameter at their widest point, you should get about 2 pints plus a 1½-pint jar from 2½ pounds of raw fruit.

# Sweet Quince Pickle

The success of this recipe depends largely on the quality and ripeness of the quinces. When they are a light golden yellow and aromatic at the time of purchase, the pickle is a joy to behold and to eat — rich, amber-colored, spicy, and full of flavor. Green quinces will ripen at home, but they make a less flavorful pickle.

I've deliberately omitted the volume of prepared fruit from the recipe because much depends on the size of the quinces you can obtain and also how you slice them. If you have no kitchen or diet scales, you can measure the prepared fruit accurately enough by standing on bathroom scales, first with a plastic bag of sliced quinces in hand and then without — just subtract the difference to estimate the weight of the fruit.

2½ to 2¾ pounds ripe quinces, peeled, cored,
   and sliced ¼ inch thick (about 2 pounds, prepared)
3¼ cups sugar
¾ cup cider vinegar
¾ cup water
½ teaspoon whole allspice
½ teaspoon whole cloves
About 8 inches stick cinnamon

  ❧ Steam the prepared quinces in a shallow layer in a covered steamer 15 to 20 minutes, or until a toothpick or small skewer pierces the slices easily. If your steamer is small, cook the fruit in two or more batches; accumulate cooked fruit in a bowl of at least 2½-quart capacity.

While the fruit cooks, assemble the syrup ingredients in a 1½-quart saucepan. Place the sugar, vinegar, and water in it. Place allspice and cloves in a metal tea ball, and add it and the cinnamon to the pan. When all the fruit is cooked, bring the syrup to a boil, stirring, and then boil rapidly without stirring for 5 minutes. Pour, boiling hot, over quince slices, and weight them with a saucer or small dish and a jar of water. As the mixture cools, the syrup will gradually cover the fruit. Let stand, uncovered, 12 hours or overnight.

The next day, turn the mixture into a wide 4-quart saucepan, bring quickly to boil, stirring occasionally, and boil rapidly 20 to 25 minutes, or until quinces look almost transparent, syrup is rosy, and jell tests done. Remove from heat, stir and skim, if necessary, about 5 minutes to cool slightly and prevent floating fruit. Pack at once in hot, sterilized half-pint jars or glasses, and seal. Makes about 4 cups, and it's just as good after one year as after one day.

# Cantaloupe Pickle

I like a sprinkling of ground ginger on chilled cantaloupe or melon balls, so I tried the same flavor combination for this old-fashioned fruit pickle. It makes a beautiful garnish for roast pork or lamb and a wonderfully spicy dressing for fruit or poultry salads. Just thin some mayonnaise, sour cream, or yogurt with a little of the syrup and add a bit of chopped melon—either mixing it into the dressing or garnishing the top if you serve it separately.

> 1 tablespoon calcium hydroxide U.S.P. (see page 201), dissolved as label directs but in only 2 quarts water
> 6 cups cubes (1-inch) firm, unripe cantaloupe
> 3 cups sugar
> 2 to 4 tablespoons, packed, finely grated crystallized ginger (about 1½ to 3 ounces)
> 1½ cups cider vinegar

🍓 Mix the calcium hydroxide solution in a 4-quart bowl (not aluminum) an hour before you are ready to use it.

Halve the melon or melons (buy at least 3 pounds) from stem end to blossom end and discard seeds. Cut halves crosswise into 1-inch slices and pare them thinly, removing just the netted skin and leaving a thin layer of green flesh, if possible. I find the curved, serrated blade of a grapefruit knife does the best job both for peeling and for trimming away soft flesh surrounding the seed cavity. Cut the strips into cubes and measure. Add cubes all at once to the calcium hydroxide solution and let stand about 4 hours.

Drain, rinse in a colander, and drain again. Rinse the bowl, return cantaloupe to it, cover with fresh water and let stand 2 hours.

Drain cantaloupe thoroughly. Place in a wide 4-quart saucepan, add remaining ingredients, and stir to dissolve sugar. Weight with a plate to keep fruit submerged, and let stand 18 to 24 hours. Refrigerate only if room is very hot.

The next day, bring to a boil quickly and adjust heat to boil steadily about 1¼ hours, or until cubes look opaque and syrup has reduced. If too much liquid has boiled away after 45 minutes, add ¼ cup water.

Spoon cubes into hot, sterilized half-pint jars within ½ to ¾ inch of top. Bring syrup to full boil and fill jars almost to overflowing. Clean rims and threads and seal. Store at least a month. Makes about 4 cups.

# Pineapple Chutney

This is totally different from traditional sweet, hot mango chutney. It is more sharp than sweet, steeped in thin syrup instead of thick, and spiced with green peppercorns instead of chilies. I first tasted a jar of it put out by a famous Paris food store; it cost the exorbitant sum of four dollars for less than eight ounces. So I worked out my own version, which not only is much cheaper but, frankly, tastes better. It has a fresher, livelier flavor. Rather than serve the chutney only with curry dishes, I offer it with roast duck and goose, pork and ham, or use it to make sauce for ham steak.

Bottle any leftover syrup to use for thinning mayonnaise for fruit salads. Or, if the quantity remaining is large, pour it over dried fruit, bring to a boil, cover, and let stand until the fruit is plump, to make a quick refrigerator compote to go with meat or poultry.

> 4 to 5 cups (¼-inch-thick wedges) fully ripe
>     pineapple (about 4½ pounds before
>     preparing)
> 2 tablespoons coarse (kosher) salt or 4
>     teaspoons table salt or pickling salt
> 1 cup sugar
> 1 cup white vinegar or white wine vinegar
> ½ cup dried currants
> 2 tablespoons whole mustard seed
> 2 tablespoons canned or bottled green
>     peppercorns, drained, rinsed, drained again,
>     and mashed slightly

Peel and core pineapple and cut into wedges. Mix pineapple with salt, and place in a colander or large strainer set over a deep bowl or pot (not aluminum). Let stand 1 hour. Discard brine, rinse pineapple in cool water to remove excess salt, and drain well.

Place sugar and vinegar in a wide 2½-quart saucepan and bring to boil quickly, stirring to dissolve sugar. Add currants, mustard seed, and peppercorns to syrup. Then add pineapple with a slotted spoon, shaking it first so any salty liquid remaining will not go into the pan. Stir to mix, and continue cooking only until fruit is thoroughly hot. Taste a piece to be sure.

Adjust heat to keep mixture hot but not boiling, and quickly spoon it into hot, sterilized half-pint or pint jars, making sure syrup covers the solids by about ¼ inch and leaving as much head space in each jar. Strain out the spices (some tend to float, and others sink), and divide them among the jars. Seal and store at least 1 month. Makes about 5 cups.

# Green Tomato Chutney

Vincent and Georgiana Banks, from whose English recipe mine is adapted, called for shallots in this peppery chutney, and I do think shallots make a superior relish. But if they are hard to find or too expensive, by all means substitute small pickling onions. Shallots can be ordered by mail (see source list, page 201); they also are as easy to grow as onion sets, by planting, root end down, one inch deep, and covering with half an inch of soil. They should be set about 8 inches apart and tended as you would onions. They can be used fresh in summer and hung upside down in a warm room to dry for winter use. I don't recommend freezing; like onions, whole shallots tend to become spongy when thawed.

2 pounds green tomatoes, cut in ½-inch dice
   (5¾ to 6 cups)
½ pound tart green apples, peeled, cored, and
   diced (about 2 cups)
½ cup, packed, golden raisins
1 cup, packed, dark brown sugar
1 tablespoon grated crystallized ginger
6 dried chili peppers (1 inch long), broken
   (remove some seeds if you want a less spicy
   product), or 1 teaspoon dried crushed red
   pepper
1½ teaspoons minced garlic (about 3 medium
   cloves)
½ pound peeled shallots or peeled pickling
   onions (less than 1 inch diameter), halved if
   large (about 1½ cups) or 3 medium onions,
   cut in ½-inch dice
1¼ cups cider vinegar

🌰 Place all the ingredients in a wide 4-quart saucepan, bring to
boil quickly, adjust heat, and boil about 30 minutes, or until as thick
as jam. Stir occasionally, to prevent sticking. Spoon into hot, sterilized half-pint jars, and seal. Let stand at least a month. Makes about
6½ cups.

# Naturally Sweet
# Nectarine Chutney

The only refined sugar in this relish is the little used in manufacturing crystallized ginger, and even the excess there should be rinsed off before you grate the confection. The nectarines and orange juice provide all the sweetening you need. I serve the chutney with curry, of course, but I also like it with roast turkey instead of cranberry sauce, and with cold roast pork and ham.

2 cups fresh orange juice
½ cup white wine vinegar or white vinegar
1½ pounds firm, ripe, unpeeled nectarines,
   washed, dried, pitted, and sliced thinly
2½ cups, packed (a 15-ounce box) golden raisins
½ pound red onions, peeled and diced (about
   2 cups)
2 to 2½ inches stick cinnamon
3 tablespoons (about 2 ounces) grated,
   crystallized ginger, rinsed to remove excess
   sugar before grating, or ½ teaspoon ground
   ginger
¼ teaspoon dried crushed red pepper
1 teaspoon salt
½ teaspoon ground mace
½ cup blanched almonds, halved

&#x1F5D5;Place all the ingredients except almonds in a wide 4-quart saucepan. Bring to boil over medium heat; adjust heat to boil slowly about 40 minutes. Stir occasionally at first, more often during the last 15 minutes, to prevent sticking. Stir in almonds, and boil, stirring, 5 minutes more. Spoon at once into hot, sterilized half-pint jars, and seal. Store at least a month. Makes about 7 cups.

# Banana Chutney

An English recipe, this chutney called for ground ginger original-ly, plus cayenne. I prefer finely cut or grated crystallized ginger and dried crushed red pepper instead. It is a sharp, spicy relish that tends to stick to the pan in the last stages of cooking; it helps to use a pan with nonstick coating.

The muscat raisins will cut or chop easier if they're frozen. Their winy flavor is more distinctive than that of golden raisins.

1¾ cups white vinegar
6 firm ripe bananas (about 2 pounds)
1 large tart apple (6 to 7 ounces or 3 inches
    diameter), peeled, cored, and chopped finely
1 small (about 2½ inches diameter) yellow
    onion, peeled and chopped finely
⅓ cup, packed, finely cut muscat raisins or
    whole golden raisins
¾ cup, packed, light brown sugar
1½ tablespoons grated crystallized ginger
    (about 1 ounce)
½ teaspoon dried crushed red pepper
½ teaspoon uniodized table salt or pickling
    salt

❧Place vinegar in wide 2½-quart saucepan. Peel bananas, and dice them directly into vinegar, stirring to coat and prevent darkening. Stir in chopped apple.

Add remaining ingredients, and bring to boil over medium heat, stirring. Lower heat and simmer 20 to 30 minutes, or until thick, stir-ring occasionally to prevent sticking.

Spoon into hot, sterilized half-pint jars and seal at once. Store at least 1 month before using; like all chutneys, it improves with even greater age. Makes 4 to 5 cups.

# Dried Apricot Chutney

An English recipe which I have made less sweet; in fact, my version is tart enough to serve with meat and poultry.

If you substitute powdered ginger for the preserved or crystallized variety, use a much smaller quantity—perhaps only 1 teaspoonful—and don't expect as good a flavor in the finished product.

11 ounces (1 package) dried apricots
1¼ cups boiling water
1 cup, packed, light brown sugar
½ pound (4 small) yellow onions, peeled,
    thinly sliced, and separated into rings
2 tablespoons finely grated preserved ginger or
    crystallized ginger
1 cup red wine vinegar
2 teaspoons dried coriander seeds, coarsely
    crushed
2 medium cloves garlic, peeled and thinly
    sliced

Place apricots in small heatproof bowl, cover with boiling water, and let stand 20 minutes.

Drain apricots well, reserving soaking liquid. Boil it down rapidly in a small saucepan until you have about 2 tablespoons of syrup.

Place the syrup with the apricots and remaining ingredients in a wide 2½-quart saucepan. Bring to boil over medium heat, lower heat, and boil slowly about 30 minutes, stirring occasionally.

Use slotted spoon to divide solids among hot, sterilized half-pint jars; cover within ¼ inch of jar rim with syrup and seal at once. Store at least 3 weeks. Makes about 3 cups.

# Blueberry Chutney

This unusual relish is particularly good with pork and ham. Mixed with mayonnaise or plain yogurt, it makes a piquant dressing for fruit salad or cold meat salads.

2 pounds, or dry pints, ripe blueberries,
   washed, well drained, sorted, stemmed, and
   lightly crushed (about 7 cups)
1½ cups red wine vinegar
¼ pound (1 medium) onion, peeled and finely
   chopped (about ½ cup)
½ cup golden raisins
½ cup, packed, light brown sugar
2 teaspoons yellow mustard seed
1 tablespoon grated crystallized ginger
½ teaspoon ground cinnamon
Pinch each of salt and ground nutmeg
½ teaspoon dried crushed red pepper

🥄 Place all ingredients in a wide 4-quart saucepan. Bring to boil over medium heat, stirring often. Boil steadily, stirring occasionally, until thick—about 45 minutes. Spoon into hot, sterilized half-pint jars, and seal. Store about a month before serving. Makes about 4 cups.

# Country Chutney

This relish is based on a prize-winning English recipe of more than a generation ago. It is less sweet than traditional chutneys; most of its sweetness comes not from sugar, but from apples, dates, and parsnips. I generally use Winesap apples but any well-flavored, crisp eating apple will do.

1¼ pounds parsnips
1 pound (3 medium) apples, peeled, cored, and sliced
½ pound (2 medium) onions, peeled and chopped (about 1 cup)
½ pound (2 medium) ripe tomatoes, peeled and finely chopped (about 1 cup)
½ teaspoon dried cracked ginger or 1 piece (1-inch) dried whole ginger
1 teaspoon mustard seed
2¼ cups cider vinegar
1 cup, packed, dark brown sugar
1 cup (4 ounces) lightly packed, dried currants
½ cup (4 ounces) packed, finely cut pitted dates
¼ cup (about 2 ounces) packed, finely diced crystallized ginger
1 teaspoon table salt
1 large pinch cayenne

❧ Cook the unpeeled parsnips 30 to 40 minutes in boiling water, to cover, in a saucepan or skillet wide enough to permit them to lie flat. They should be soft enough to mash. When the parsnips can be pierced easily with a fork, drain and cover with cold water until cool enough to handle. Peel and mash.

Simmer the apple slices with ½ cup water in a covered 1½-quart saucepan 12 to 15 minutes, or until soft enough to mash. Do not drain.

Place the mashed parsnips and apples in a wide 4-quart saucepan. Add onions and tomatoes; tie ginger and mustard seed loosely in a double thickness of dampened cheesecloth or place in a metal tea ball and add to the pan, along with vinegar. Bring to boil over medium heat and simmer slowly 1 hour, stirring occasionally.

Add remaining ingredients and simmer 1 hour more, or until thick. Stir occasionally to prevent sticking. The chutney will darken considerably.

Remove from heat and spoon at once into hot, sterilized half-pint or pint jars and seal. Store at least 1 month before opening. Makes about 7 cups.

# Icebox Pickles
## and Relishes

# Quick Dill Slices

I make these whenever I have a windfall from gardening friends and no time or not enough cucumbers to put up winter pickles or relish. They keep almost indefinitely in the refrigerator, and while they can be eaten at once, they're milder when they're a few weeks old. They go beautifully with fish or cold meat loaf.

The measurements are only approximations. And you can add some thinly sliced mild onions if you like. If you pack the pickles in an attractive, tightly stoppered apothecary jar, you can serve straight from it at the table.

> About 1½ pounds unwaxed cucumbers, thinly
>   sliced
> 1 tablespoon table salt
> Several sprigs fresh dill or about 2 teaspoons
>   dried dill weed
> White wine vinegar or rice wine vinegar or
>   cider vinegar (about 2 cups)

🍓 Layer cucumber slices with salt in a colander, and cover with a plate weighted with a heavy can or jar. Let stand about 1 hour. Then rinse to remove excess salt, drain well, and layer with the fresh or dried dill in a jar or dish you can cover tightly. Cover with vinegar and refrigerate. Makes about 1 quart.

# Mother's Pickled Beets

This sharp pickle is good with either fish or cold meats and poultry. It will keep for weeks in the refrigerator if you can hide it from raiders. When all the beets and onions have been eaten, recycle the brine by filling the jar with hard-cooked eggs. Return the jar to the refrigerator until the egg whites have turned a uniformly deep pink. They can be eaten after two days but are better after a week. Sliced or quartered, the eggs make a beautiful garnish for salads and platters of cold food.

If this pickle is too sharp for your taste, dissolve ¼ cup of sugar in a little of the vinegar over medium heat and add it to the jar when you pour the cold vinegar on. Or substitute ¼ cup water for the same amount of vinegar.

About 1 pound beets
2 onions, about 2 inches diameter, peeled and
     sliced ¼ inch thick and separated into rings
1 teaspoon salt
About 1 cup cider vinegar or red wine vinegar

Leave roots and at least 1 inch of stem on the beets to help keep their color. Scrub them well before cooking. I like to pressure cook them to retain maximum flavor, but it's almost impossible to suggest cooking time because beets vary so widely in size. Follow the manufacturer's directions for pressure cooking, or test beets with a fork if you steam or boil them in a saucepan.

Rinse the cooked beets in cool, running water only until they're cool enough to handle. Break off the roots and stems, and rub off the skin.

Slice the beets about ¼ inch thick, and pack while warm into a hot, scalded 1½-pint wide mouth jar, alternating beet slices with raw onion rings.

Add the salt, and cover with vinegar. Seal. Refrigerate as soon as the jar has cooled, and keep refrigerated at least a week — but two weeks are better. The beets are ready when the onion rings have turned a uniform deep pink.

# Mustard Sauce with Apples

Made with crisp, tart apples and sharp mustard (or the mild kind with whole seeds in it), this relish is a perfect foil for roast fresh ham, loin of pork, or roast duck or goose. Much better, I think, than the traditional apple sauce. Try it, too, with the leaner, blander meats such as turkey and chicken. My recipe is adapted from a book published in 1928 and, although I have given more specific measurements, the quantities really should be varied to suit personal tastes.

(An apple is easier to grate if you don't core it. Its stem and blossom ends make good finger grips for holding the fruit against the grater.)

1 tablespoon Dijon-type mustard or seeded
   mustard
3 tablespoons olive oil
¼ teaspoon paprika
½ teaspoon salt
1 tablespoon sugar, or more to taste
Juice of 1 medium (3 ounces) lemon
1½ teaspoons cider vinegar
3 to 4 apples, peeled and grated

🍎 Place mustard in a 3-cup mixing bowl. Gradually beat in olive oil with a fork or a wire whisk. Stir in remaining ingredients. Taste and adjust seasonings.

Refrigerate in a tightly covered container if relish will not be served at once, but bring to room temperature before serving. It will keep at least 2 months in the refrigerator, but the flavor is best when used within 1 month.

The yield varies, depending on the size of the apples used. With 2 large golden delicious and 2 small greenings, you get about 2 cups of relish. All eating apples can be used for a sweeter relish or all cooking apples for a tart one.

# Frozen Sliced Sweet Dill Pickles

These are the crispest sliced sweet pickles I have ever tasted. They are marvelous on open sandwiches of thinly sliced pumpernickel spread with cream cheese. Yet the idea of frozen pickles seemed so strange, I almost didn't try it the first time I encountered a recipe. But now I keep a supply of these pickles in the freezer at all times, particularly for people with a sweet tooth.

1 pound 3-inch unwaxed cucumbers, sliced ⅛ inch thick (about 4 cups, packed)
¾ pound 2-inch yellow onions, sliced ⅛ inch thick (about 2 cups, packed)
4 teaspoons table salt
2 tablespoons water
¾ to 1 cup sugar
½ cup cider vinegar
1 teaspoon dried dill weed (or more to taste)

🔥Mix the prepared cucumbers, onions, salt, and water in a 2-quart bowl (not aluminum), and let stand about 2 hours. Drain, but do not rinse.

Return the vegetables to the bowl, and add the sugar, the vinegar, and the dill. Let stand, stirring from time to time, until sugar has dissolved completely and liquid covers the vegetables. Pack in glass or plastic freezer containers (leave 1 inch of head space), seal tightly, and freeze. Makes about 4 cups.

Defrost either in the refrigerator or at room temperature. Defrosting time will vary greatly, depending on the size of the freezer containers and the temperature.

# Sauces, Savory and Sweet, and a Pie Filling

# Cranberry Ketchup

This rich, red, thick, and spicy sauce is just the thing to serve with cold turkey and cold roast pork. I've often wondered why it isn't produced commercially on a large scale; only occasionally in country gift shops one is apt to find bottles of it put up in limited quantities by an individual or a small company. So there's all the more reason to make your own.

3/4 pound onions, coarsely chopped or diced
  (about 2 cups)
2 pounds cranberries, sorted, washed, and well
  drained
1 1/2 cups water
1 pound light brown sugar (2 1/4 cups, packed)
1/2 teaspoon ground cloves
1 1/2 teaspoons ground cinnamon
1 teaspoon ground allspice
1/2 teaspoon ground ginger
1 teaspoon salt
1/4 teaspoon ground pepper
1 cup red wine vinegar

Place onions, cranberries, and water in a wide 4-quart saucepan, cover tightly, and boil 15 minutes, until berries have popped and onions are tender. Stir once or twice toward the end of the cooking time.

Put the mixture through a food mill until you have about 5 1/2 cups of purée. Mix sugar with spices and add, with vinegar, to the fruit. Stir to mix well, bring to a full boil, pack at once into hot, sterilized half-pint jars, and seal.

Do not overcook, or you may end up with a jelly instead of a sauce. Makes about 7 cups.

# Green Tomato Ketchup

Once upon a time English sea captains returning home from Asia brought word of a spicy condiment the Chinese called koechiap or ketsiap; the Malaysians called it kechap or kechup. It was in the seventeenth century that imitation ketchups began appearing, made from cucumbers or mushrooms or walnuts and, later, tomatoes from the Americas. The first Western ketchups resembled their Asian ancestors in name only. The Orientals used fish brine with herbs and spices, and versions of this condiment still are popular today from the Philippines to Southeast Asia. My version is based on an old American recipe devised by a Pennsylvanian to use up green tomatoes that had to be harvested before frost. It is both peppery and fruity; the tomato, apple, and onion combination makes it a good relish to serve with pork and ham, as well as with hamburgers.

1 pound onions, peeled and thinly sliced
1 pound green tomatoes, peeled and thinly sliced
1 pound tart green apples, cored and thinly sliced
1½ tablespoons coarse (kosher) salt or 1 tablespoon uniodized table salt or pickling salt
2 cups white vinegar
½ teaspoon cayenne
½ teaspoon ground cloves
½ teaspoon ground cinnamon
1 teaspoon ground mace
2 teaspoons ground mustard
¼ cup sugar
Green vegetable coloring (optional)

🌱Layer onions, tomatoes, and apples in a 1½- or 2-quart bowl (not aluminum), sprinkling each layer with some of the salt. Let stand about 12 hours, or overnight.

The next day, drain well and chop in an electric blender, using the vinegar as liquid and following the blender manufacturer's directions for quantities to be blended at one time. Drain off liquid to reuse as necessary. (If you have no blender, put the onions, tomatoes, and apples through a grinder, using the fine blade.)

Place all ingredients (except coloring), including the liquid and the vinegar, in a wide 4-quart saucepan. Bring quickly to boil, stirring once or twice. Boil steadily about 30 minutes, or until mixture is almost the consistency of bottled tomato ketchup. It will thicken more as it cools. Remove from heat and stir in a few drops of vegetable coloring to tint it a pale green. Spoon at once into hot, sterilized half-pint jars and seal. Store at least 1 month before using. Makes about 5½ cups.

# Sweet Pepper Ketchup

Either green or ripe (red) bell peppers can be used for this sauce, but red ones make a more attractive, spectacularly bright product. It is low in calories—about 15 per tablespoonful—and is just as good with fish as it is with hamburgers and cold meats. I've put it in mayonnaise for egg salad and mixed it into a blend of mayonnaise and stiffly beaten egg whites to make a topping for fish fillets to be baked.

If you cannot find ripe bell peppers at your market, look for green ones tinged with pink. Leave them in a closed paper bag in a warm spot out of direct sunlight for several days and check daily, refrigerating each pepper as soon as it's ripe.

Ripe red peppers make a prettier relish, but there's apt to be more waste in preparing them. Because they are ripe, hidden bad spots develop faster and must be cut out and discarded before you grind the peppers.

1½ teaspoons celery seed
1½ teaspoons mustard seed
2 tablespoons well-drained bottled horseradish
    or 1 tablespoon dehydrated horseradish or
    horseradish powder
1 cup red wine vinegar
3 to 3¼ pounds (12 medium) sweet red bell
    peppers, stemmed, seeded, and finely
    ground (about 7 cups)
2 small onions, about 2 inches diameter,
    peeled and finely ground
1½ teaspoons coarse (kosher) salt or 1
    teaspoon uniodized table salt or pickling salt
½ cup plus 1 tablespoon, packed, light brown
    sugar

🔔 Place celery and mustard seed, horseradish, and vinegar in a wide 4-quart saucepan while you grind the peppers and onions. Add the vegetables with their juices to the pan, along with the salt and sugar.

Bring to boil quickly over high heat, stirring. Adjust heat to retain a steady boil, and cook, stirring occasionally, about 45 minutes, until the mixture is the texture of bottled chili sauce. Ladle at once into hot, sterilized half-pint or pint jars, and seal.

It's almost impossible to predict the yield accurately, because some peppers are meatier than others, with fewer seeds in proportion to edible portions. I've gotten as little as 4½ cups from red peppers and as much as 7 cups from green ones.

# Mint Sauce

Traditional English mint sauce uses malt vinegar and fresh mint leaves, but I found quite by accident that half red wine vinegar and half cider vinegar make a more appetizing, milder blend.

    1 cup red wine vinegar
    1 cup cider vinegar
    2 cups fresh mint leaves, tightly packed
    2 to 4 tablespoons sugar or its equivalent in
        noncaloric sugar substitute—or to taste

🕯Place 1 cup of vinegar in container of an electric blender. Add half the mint and blend on high speed until mint is finely chopped. Scrape down sides of container occasionally with a rubber spatula. Empty mixture into a ¾- or 1-quart saucepan. Repeat, using remaining vinegar and mint. Add it to the saucepan. If you are using sugar, dissolve it in a tablespoon or two of boiling water and add to the saucepan. Heat to full boil, and pour at once into hot, sterilized half-pint jars and seal. Makes about 2 cups.

If you use a sugar substitute, bottle the sauce unsweetened and attach a label with directions for adding the sweetener before serving. Never add sugar substitute when the sauce is hot—some substitutes leave a bitter aftertaste in hot mixtures.

The mint flavor weakens during long storage—six months or more. You can restore its strength, if you wish, with a few drops of mint extract.

# Green Tomato and Horseradish Sauce

Sometimes old recipes can be misleading, as I learned the first time I made this sauce. It was overcooked and oversalted. And no wonder! The original recipe, in a book published almost a century ago in Canada, called for day-long cooking and a whole cup of salt! But I liked the combination of ingredients, so I worked out a version that cooks in an hour. It is particularly good with boiled fresh (or smoked) tongue and almost any kind of grilled fish.

1 pound coarsely ground green tomatoes
  (about 2 cups)
1/2 pound green peppers, stemmed, seeded,
  and coarsely ground (about 1 cup)
1 pound onions, peeled and coarsely ground
  (about 2 cups)
2 tablespoons plus 1 teaspoon coarse (kosher) salt
  or 2 tablespoons uniodized table salt or pickling salt
1 cup sugar
1/8 teaspoon ground cloves
1/2 teaspoon ground cinnamon
2 1/2 cups cider vinegar
2 bottles (6 ounces each) prepared horseradish
  packed in vinegar and salt (about 1 1/4 cups)

🍓 Mix tomatoes, peppers, onions, and salt in a 1 1/2-quart bowl (not aluminum), and let stand 8 hours or more. Then drain, rinse, and drain again. Place the vegetables in a wide 2 1/2-quart saucepan, add the sugar, spices, and vinegar, and simmer about 1 hour, or until thick. Stir occasionally. Add the horseradish during the last 5 minutes of cooking, and spoon, boiling hot, into hot, sterilized half-pint jars. Store a week or two before serving. Makes about 6 cups.

# Spicy Chili Sauce

A good relish to make when you have a bumper crop of tomatoes or when they are sale-priced at the market. It is delicious on hamburgers and even better mixed with mayonnaise to dress fish salads. Sometimes I stir it into melted butter to serve on broiled fish fillets or steaks.

$6\frac{1}{2}$ pounds firm, ripe tomatoes, peeled and
    cut into $\frac{3}{4}$-inch chunks (10 to 11 cups)
$\frac{1}{2}$ pound (3 medium) onions, peeled and
    chopped finely (about 1 cup)
$\frac{3}{4}$ pound red or green bell peppers, stemmed,
    seeded, and chopped finely ($\frac{3}{4}$ to 1 cup)
2 cups cider vinegar
$\frac{1}{2}$ cup sugar
$\frac{1}{4}$ teaspoon cayenne
$\frac{1}{2}$ teaspoon ground mustard
$1\frac{1}{2}$ teaspoons celery seed
$1\frac{1}{2}$ teaspoons ground cinnamon
$\frac{1}{2}$ teaspoon ground mace
$\frac{1}{2}$ teaspoon ground cloves
2 teaspoons salt

❦Place all ingredients in a wide 4-quart saucepan, bring quickly to boil, and simmer about $3\frac{1}{2}$ hours, or until slightly thicker than ketchup. Stir often, especially toward end of the cooking time, to prevent sticking. Spoon into hot, sterilized half-pint jars, and seal. Makes about 6 cups.

# Sweet-and-Sour Duck Sauce

Duck sauce, sometimes called plum sauce, came to the United States from China, where it is a spicy, reddish brown condiment to be eaten with duck, of course. It isn't necessarily made with plums — some sauces contain apricots, peaches, or plums or combinations of these fruits. My version is a fine dipping sauce not just for roast duck, but also for barbecued spareribs. I also like to mix it with oil and vinegar to glaze spareribs or duckling during the last 20 to 30 minutes of roasting or grilling.

3 pounds firm, ripe red plums, pitted and cut
   into ½-inch chunks (about 2 quarts)
½ teaspoon peeled, crushed garlic
½ pound onions, peeled and finely chopped
   (about 1 cup)
1 cup rice wine vinegar or cider vinegar
½ teaspoon dried crushed red pepper
1 teaspoon ground coriander
½ teaspoon ground allspice
2½ cups sugar

Place all the ingredients except the sugar in a wide 4-quart saucepan and bring to boil over medium heat, stirring occasionally. Boil steadily about 30 minutes.

Remove from heat, put through food mill, and return puréed fruit to pan. Add sugar, place over medium heat, and stir constantly until mixture again boils. Boil steadily about 30 minutes, stirring often to prevent sticking; continue boiling about 15 minutes more, stirring constantly. Sauce is done when about ½ teaspoon of it holds its shape on a chilled saucer. Spoon at once into hot, sterilized half-pint jars and seal. Store at least a week to mellow. Makes about 5½ cups.

# Blueberry-Orange Sauce

This quick, easy, and lightly sweetened sauce has many uses: it is good over ice cream and pound cake, but it is especially delicious with crêpes or over fresh, unsweetened fruit—particularly blueberries, strawberries, peaches, or nectarines.

1 pound, or dry pint, fresh, ripe blueberries,
    washed, well drained, stemmed, and slightly
    crushed (about 7 cups)
²/₃ cup sugar
¼ teaspoon salt
2 teaspoons grated fresh orange peel
2 tablespoons orange-flavored liqueur or 1
    teaspoon orange extract

&#9827;Place berries, sugar, salt, and grated peel in a 1½-quart saucepan over low heat, and stir until juices start to flow. Increase heat, bring mixture to boil, and boil hard 1 minute. Remove from heat, stir in liqueur or extract, and spoon at once into hot, scalded half-pint or 4-ounce jars. Seal, cool, and refrigerate. It can be served the day it's made but is better if allowed to mellow about a week. Makes about 2½ cups.

# Pineapple-Rhubarb Sauce

This pale pink dessert sauce is refreshingly tart with lemon souf-flé. It is also good with pancakes, waffles, French toast, ice cream, and fresh fruit. I sometimes use it to thin mayonnaise for fruit salad. If you keep it more than a couple of months, you may find its color darkening unappetizingly, but the flavor holds up well. I sometimes stir in a few drops of red vegetable coloring to correct the color.

4 cups diced fresh pineapple (4½ to 5 pound
    fruit or 2 smaller ones)
2 pounds rhubarb, diced (about 7 cups); discard leaves
3½ cups sugar
¼ cup lemon juice (reserve seeds)

Peel, core and dice pineapple. Place pineapple and rhubarb in a wide 4-quart saucepan, and bring to boil over medium heat, stirring often. Cook, stirring occasionally, 15 to 20 minutes, or until fruit is soft enough to put through a food mill into a bowl of at least 1½-quart capacity. You should have about 4½ cups of purée. Return it to the saucepan, add sugar and lemon juice, and stir until dissolved. Place lemon seeds in a metal tea ball or tie them loosely in two thicknesses of dampened cheesecloth, and drop into sauce. Bring to boil quickly, and boil rapidly 15 minutes, stirring occasionally.

Remove from heat, skim if necessary, pour into hot, sterilized half-pint jars, and seal at once. Makes about 5½ cups.

# Spiced Brandied Chestnuts

If you've ever wondered why brandied chestnuts are so expensive, you'll know when you shell the nuts for this delectable ice cream sauce. Shelling is tedious, time-consuming labor, but well worth the effort if you like the rich flavor and velvety texture of chestnuts as much as I do. With brandied or plain marrons in syrup selling for about ten dollars for an 8- or 9-ounce jar, the homemade kind is a bargain even if you must pay almost a dollar a pound for the fresh nuts. Incidentally, I've found that freezing the chestnuts for at least 24 hours makes them easier to shell and peel. Fresh unshelled chestnuts will keep refrigerated for a few weeks, and for months in the freezer. In either case, they should be in an airtight container. (Although I have specified 2 pounds of nuts, I usually buy an extra ¼ or ½ pound to make up for possible spoilage.)

2 to 2¼ pounds (about 6 cups) small or
    medium unshelled chestnuts
4 cups, packed, light brown sugar
1½ cups brandy
1 teaspoon freshly grated nutmeg or about 4
    inches vanilla bean

❦ If you have frozen the chestnuts, thaw them at room temperature in a single layer on shallow trays. This probably will take 2 hours or more. When the nuts are at room temperature, place them in a wide 2½-quart saucepan and cover with boiling water at least 2 inches above the surface of the nuts. Cover pan tightly, and let stand 5 minutes for thawed nuts or 10 minutes for nuts that have not been frozen.

Fish out two or three nuts at a time and use the tip of a very sharp, small knife to strip off the shell and the inner peel. I find it easiest to pierce the nuts first on their flat sides and peel off the flexible shell, starting at the pointed tip. Be sure to pry out bits of skin in the crevices. Sometimes you will have to break a nut to do this, but try to keep them as whole as possible.

Because their oil content is low and the starch content high, chestnuts mold easily, and the mold often is invisible until the nuts are cleaned. Be sure to cut away even the slightest trace of mold; otherwise it could ruin the entire batch. Also discard nutmeats that are blackish or otherwise discolored.

As you near the end of the batch, you may have to return some nuts to the water and reheat them briefly to peel stubborn spots. When all the nuts are ready, either preserve them at once or refrigerate them, tightly covered, for no more than two days.

To preserve the nuts, place them in a wide 2½-quart saucepan, cover with 4 cups of boiling water, cover pan, and simmer 25 to 30 minutes, or until nuts are tender. It is important that they simmer instead of boil; otherwise they may break up entirely. Drain, reserving 1½ cups of the cooking water; leave the nuts in the pan.

In a 2-quart saucepan, combine the reserved water with brown sugar, brandy, and nutmeg or vanilla bean. Bring to boil, stirring; continue to boil rapidly 15 minutes. Pour the syrup over the nuts and return pan to heat until syrup boils again. Reduce heat to keep syrup hot but not simmering; use a slotted spoon to divide nuts among 8 hot, sterilized half-pint jars, filling each about three-fourths full. Divide the syrup among the jars, filling each within about ¼ inch of top. If you have used vanilla bean, cut it into ½-inch lengths and drop one piece into each jar. Clean rims and threads and seal. The chestnuts will float at first, then sink as they absorb syrup. Store a week or two before using. Makes about 8 cups.

# Spiced Brandied Fruit Sauce

A Christmas gift of imported French glacé cherries in brandy reminded me that holiday cakes made with brandied preserved fruit would be particularly delicious, and far less expensive to make if I brandied the fruit at home. My sauce is also good over ice cream, and a little of it is delicious in stuffing for roast duck or goose.

If you like raisins, add ½ cup to the glacé fruit and increase brandy so all the solids are covered.

    1 jar or package (1 pound) glacé mixed, diced
        fruit and peels (about 2 cups)
    ¼ cup diced crystallized ginger
    ½ teaspoon whole allspice
    ½ teaspoon whole cloves
    About 5 inches stick cinnamon
    1½ cups brandy

🥄 Mix the fruit with the ginger in a clean, scalded 1-quart canning jar or an apothecary jar with a tight lid. Place the allspice and cloves in a metal tea ball, and bury it and the cinnamon in the fruit.

Cover fruit with brandy, and seal jar. After 3 weeks, taste a piece of fruit. If it is spicy enough to suit you, discard the spices and reseal the jar. If not, leave the spices a while longer. The sauce keeps indefinitely. Makes slightly more than 3 cups.

# Grape Pie Filling

In my childhood, Concord grape pie was a dessert we had often in September and October, when the grapes ripened. My brothers and I loved the sharp yet sweet filling inside Mother's marvelously flaky pastry, and we never ceased to be amused by the side effect: our tongues and lips dyed purple for a while after eating.

When I moved to New York, I found I could buy 3-pound baskets of Concord grapes each fall at vegetable stands and a few fancy food markets, and I started canning enough each year to make two or three pies when the mood suited me. I've never had a jar of filling spoil, but once in a while I've forgotten one at the back of a shelf and found it more than a year later, the contents faded but edible. Directions for the pie follow the filling recipe.

> 2-quart basket (about 3 pounds) fully ripe
>    Concord grapes
> 1 pound (1 box) light brown sugar

&#x2767; Wash grapes and drain well. Slip pulp from skins into a wide 2½-quart saucepan, and reserve the skins in a 1-quart bowl.

Bring pulp to boil over medium heat, stirring. Boil about 10 minutes, or until seeds begin to separate from pulp. Remove from heat and strain, pushing with wooden spoon to extract as much pulp as possible. Return pulp to pan, add sugar and skins, and bring to boil. Boil rapidly, stirring once or twice, about 5 minutes, until sugar dissolves and mixture looks glossy. Ladle at once into a hot, sterilized 1½-pint jar and a 1-pint jar, and seal.

The larger jar holds enough for a 9-inch pie and the smaller one for an 8-inch pie.

# GRAPE PIE

Pastry for 8-inch or 9-inch pie, single or
double crust

**For 8-inch pie**

2 cups grape pie filling (preceding recipe)
2 tablespoons flour or 1 tablespoon cornstarch

**For 9-inch pie**

3 cups grape pie filling (preceding recipe)
¼ cup flour or 2 tablespoons cornstarch

Preheat the oven to 425 degrees.

Line a pie pan with pastry, and flute the edges.

In a custard cup, stir a few spoonfuls of pie filling into the flour
or cornstarch until no lumps remain, then stir this mixture into the
remaining filling. Pour into the crust, and top with a lattice crust or
bake as is—about 30 to 35 minutes, or until the edges and top crust, if
any, are brown. Serve at room temperature with pouring cream or vanilla ice cream. Or place a thin slice of natural cheddar cheese on
each wedge and warm in a 350-degree oven only long enough to melt
the cheese slightly. An 8-inch pie makes 4 to 5 servings; the 9-inch one,
5 to 6. The filling should be a little runny.

# A Miscellany
# (Beverages, Conserves, Compotes, and Condiments)

# Garapina

This light, refreshing beverage is made with unlikely ingredients—pineapple peelings and core. I first came across it in a Puerto Rican cookbook that gave no measurements. After experimenting a bit, I came up with this delicately flavored drink. It tastes best well chilled and served over ice, with a stick of fresh pineapple as stirrer.

The core and washed rind of a 4 to 4½-pound
   ripe pineapple, the rind cut in chunks, the
   core ground
4 cups water
Sugar

🐚 Place the rind, core, and water in a mixing bowl or a large bottle or a pitcher of at least 2-quart capacity. Cover with plastic wrap or cheesecloth and let stand until mixture begins to ferment. This can take as little as 24 hours in summer.

When the bubbles of fermentation begin rising, strain the mixture through dampened cheesecloth, sweeten to taste—about 2 tablespoons of sugar or the equivalent in sugar substitute should be enough—funnel the drink into a bottle, cover, and refrigerate. Makes about 1 quart.

# Orange-Flavored Sherry

Both oranges and sherry are a felicitous part of our Spanish heritage. The idea of combining them came to me when someone told me about an orange-flavored sherry from Spain. I never did locate a bottle of it, and my homemade version tastes so good I have stopped looking for the imported kind. I like to serve this sherry in true Spanish fashion, accompanied by toasted or salted almonds.

Thinly pared peel of 2 medium oranges
1 bottle (fifth) of good quality dry sherry

☙ Use a swivel-blade vegetable peeler to remove strips of peel as thinly as possible from the oranges. Decant the sherry into a clean, scalded, glass-topped quart Mason jar or an apothecary jar. Twist each strip of peel over the surface of the wine to release the oil that carries the flavor. Drop the peel into the wine, seal the jar, and store for at least a month in a cool, dark, dry place. Decant into a pretty jar with a tight stopper, and serve, chilled or over ice, with a thin half-slice of fresh orange or a twist of orange peel. Or pour a few spoonfuls over fresh fruit an hour or so before serving.

# Jasmine Markarian's Apricot Cordial

The apricot's botanical name is *Prunus armeniaca*, which may explain why some people have attributed its origin to Armenia in western Asia. But most experts agree that the luscious peach-colored fruit first grew in China and spread westward from there, eventually reaching California. It is probably no accident that the San Joaquin Valley there has both an Armenian-American colony and apricot orchards. Jasmine is a member of that colony, and this is how she describes making the delectable beverage she makes from dried apricots at her home in Fresno:

"Choose a glass jar with cover. Place alternating layers — 1 inch — of dried apricots and rock candy to within 1½ inches from top. Choose very flavorful apricots (important). Fill jar with an inexpensive brand of vodka. Close jar tightly, and place in a cupboard or on kitchen drainboard.

"After one month, open jar, taste for sweetness, and if necessary add more rock candy. Stir well but carefully with a wooden spoon. Close again, and after one month repeat procedure. After one more month (three months in all) drain into decanter.

"If the apricots are flavorful and meaty they may be used over again (I might add some fresh dried ones)."

Jasmine uses the drained apricots in sweet breads and fruit cake or chopped and served with a little of the cordial as a topping for rich vanilla ice cream. To keep the drained fruit for several months, refrigerate it in a tightly closed container.

Here is my version; as a beverage it is delicious alone or mixed with brandy.

About ¾ pound dried apricots
About ¾ pound rock candy
About 2 cups 80-proof vodka

&#x1F34A; Fill a clean, scalded, glass-topped quart Mason jar or apothecary jar with alternating layers of apricots and rock candy, starting with an inch-thick layer of apricots, lightly packed. Cover mixture with the vodka, seal tightly, and set aside for 3 months. Taste for sweetness (and adjust it, if you wish) at the end of the first month. Stir the mixture, recap it, and repeat the procedure at the end of the second month. After the third, strain the cordial into a decanter of at least 2-cup capacity, cover, and store at room temperature. I follow Jasmine's suggestions for storing and using the drained fruit. Because most of the apricot flavor has gone into the cordial, the fruit does not make good preserves or apricot butter.

# Ratafia de Figues

Ratafias are homemade liqueurs that were popular a century and more ago. They were made with all manner of things—freshly roasted coffee or cocoa beans, fruit, fruit peel and leaves, flowers, and herbs. Most of the old ratafias were based on brandy or pure grain alcohol. I find brandy works best with most fruit except for dried apricots, which have enough flavor of their own to transform tasteless vodka into nectar. This ratafia, like the preceding one for Jasmine Markarian's apricot cordial, can be used as a sauce for ice cream as well as an after-dinner drink. As a beverage, it tastes best mixed with additional brandy.

12 ounces (1 package) dried figs
½ pound rock candy or 1 cup plus 2
   tablespoons sugar
1¼ cups brandy

Place all ingredients in a clean, scalded, glass-topped quart Mason jar or apothecary jar, and seal. Let stand 3 months. Stir or shake occasionally to dissolve the rock candy or sugar; the latter tends to settle. Taste after 1 month and add more sweetening, if you wish, but remember that dried figs are extremely sweet.

Decant ratafia into a clean, scalded bottle of 10- to 12-ounce capacity, and seal tightly. Refrigerate the figs in a tightly covered, rigid container. To serve as sauce, offer the fruit, cut up, in a few spoonfuls of the syrupy cordial.

# Ponche Crema

*Ponche crema* is Spanish for cream punch. It is so thick it is served, traditionally, in tiny glasses and eaten with a spoon. Demitasse cups make a pretty and practical substitute for glasses. I also like to serve the punch as a dip for fresh ripe fruit, especially dark sweet cherries and chunks of pineapple, peaches, nectarines, pears, and melon. Cream punches are popular throughout the West Indies, and this particular version is from Curaçao. I came across it in an interesting little collection from the Netherlands Antilles, *This is the Way We Cook!*, compiled and illustrated by Jewell Fenzi and Helen Dovale.

2 tablespoons plus about 1⅓ cups white or
  light rum
1 teaspoon freshly grated nutmeg
3 whole eggs
3 egg yolks
1⅓ cups (a 14-ounce can) condensed milk
⅔ cup (a 5⅓-ounce can) evaporated milk
1 teaspoon vanilla extract

❧Place the 2 tablespoons of rum and the nutmeg in a small glass or custard cup, and set aside. Beat eggs and extra yolks together with a wire whisk in a large mixing bowl until light and frothy.

Add condensed milk, scraping the can with a rubber spatula to remove all the milk. Beat it into the eggs thoroughly.

Use milk can to measure remaining rum; beat rum into the egg-milk mixture. Add evaporated milk, and beat again until blended. Strain the nutmeg-flavored rum into the *ponche* through a tea strainer lined with 2 or 3 thicknesses of damp cheesecloth. Stir in the vanilla.

Place *ponche* in top half of a 1½-quart double boiler or a metal mixing bowl (not aluminum) set in a saucepan that will hold the bottom of the bowl above water level. Cook over hot, but not boiling, water, and stir constantly with a wire whisk for about 15 minutes, or until mixture thickens.

When *ponche* is thick, remove the pan or bowl immediately to a large pot or sink filled with ice cubes and water. Continue to whisk the mixture constantly until it reaches room temperature.

Pour into a sterilized quart jar, seal, and refrigerate. When it is well chilled, you can freeze it in a can-and-freeze type of Mason jar. Leave at least 1 inch of head space in jar. The punch will not crystallize or freeze as solidly as ice cream because of its high sugar and alcoholic content. For the same reason, it defrosts rapidly at room temperature. Mrs. Fenzi says it keeps indefinitely when refrigerated.

Don't be tempted to substitute fresh milk or cream for the evaporated milk. It won't change the flavor, but it could affect keeping quality. Makes about 1 quart.

# Nectarine-Honeydew Conserve

An unusual dessert sauce, this fruit and nut conserve is also delicious with popovers and other hot breads. You might also make it with peaches and cantaloupe instead of nectarines and honeydew.

1½ pounds semiripe nectarines, peeled, pitted,
    and cut in ½-inch dice (about 3½ cups)
Finely grated peel of 2 medium oranges
½ cup orange juice
About half a 3¼-pound firm honeydew melon,
    preferably slightly underripe, cut in ½-inch
    cubes (5 cups)
3 cups sugar
½ cup blanched, shredded almonds

Place nectarines, orange peel, and juice in a wide 2½-quart saucepan, and bring to boil quickly, stirring. Cover tightly, and reduce heat so mixture boils slowly 10 to 15 minutes, or until fruit is tender when pierced with a toothpick. Stir often to prevent sticking.

Remove from heat and add honeydew, sugar, and nuts all at once. Return to heat, and bring to boil, stirring to dissolve sugar. Boil steadily about 10 minutes, until honeydew changes from bright to pale green.

Remove from heat and pour into a colander over a heatproof bowl. Let drain thoroughly, then return syrup to pan and boil rapidly about 10 minutes, or until thick and reduced by about half. Return fruit to the pan along with any syrup remaining in the bowl. Heat to boiling, spoon into hot, sterilized half-pint jars, and seal. Store at least a week. Makes 4 to 5 cups.

# Essence of Peach

The relatively low sugar content of this conserve seems to intensify the peach flavor, and the tartness makes it a delicious foil for salt meat—ham or corned beef—or rich dishes such as pork, duck, and goose.

    2 quarts peeled, pitted, sliced ripe peaches
        (about 3 1/2 to 4 pounds before preparing)
    3 tablespoons ascorbic acid mixture (page 201)
        or 1 tablespoon each of vinegar and salt
        dissolved in 2 quarts cold water
    1 cup light, or golden, raisins
    1 1/4 cups sugar
    3/4 cup fresh lemon juice
    2 teaspoons whole mustard seed
    4 inches stick cinnamon, broken
    1/2 teaspoon whole cloves
    1/2 cup coarsely broken walnuts, blanched 5
        minutes in boiling water to prevent
        darkening
    1 tablespoon brandy per half-pint jar

When you slice peaches, put them directly into a 4-quart bowl containing the ascorbic acid mixture or acidulated water to prevent darkening. Do not use an aluminum bowl if the water contains salt. When all the fruit is prepared, drain it thoroughly (and rinse and drain again if you have used the vinegar-salt mixture). Place peaches in a wide 4-quart saucepan with raisins, sugar, and lemon juice. Tie spices loosely in a double thickness of dampened cheesecloth or place in a metal tea ball (if you like, the mustard seed can be added directly to the fruit) and add to saucepan. Place over low heat until juices start to flow. Raise heat slightly, and cook, stirring occasionally, about 45 minutes, or until conserve thickens slightly.

Remove from heat, discard spices, stir in nuts, and ladle immediately into hot, sterilized half-pint jars within ½ inch of top. Add 1 tablespoon brandy to each jar, and seal. The just-cooked relish has a sharp, tart flavor that may tempt you to add more sugar. Don't. The conserve mellows as it ages, and additional sugar would make it more like a sweet preserve. Store at least 3 weeks and chill before serving. Makes 3 to 4 cups.

# Cherry Compote

The natural spiciness of fresh sour pie cherries is as irresistible for me as the fragrance of a fully ripe pineapple, and it is quite apparent in this lightly sweetened compote. I've given two sugar measurements, the smaller one to be used if you plan to serve the compote with the main course instead of dessert. As a dessert, I like the cherries and a spoonful or two of their sauce over vanilla ice cream or toasted pound cake. They are marvelous on cheese cake, too, if you drain the cherries well and thicken their sauce with cornstarch or arrowroot.

2 pounds ripe red sour cherries, stemmed and
  pitted
⅔ to 1 cup sugar
2 teaspoons vanilla brandy (page 188)

Mix cherries and sugar in a 1½-quart saucepan. Let stand at least 30 minutes, until syrup starts to form. Simmer 8 to 9 minutes. Stir occasionally. Remove from heat, and stir in vanilla brandy. Cool, cover, and refrigerate. Makes about 2⅔ cups.

# Dried Fruit Compote

A preserve to make any time of year, this compote is not too sweet to serve with roast meat and fowl. I like the apricot variety best, but the mixed dried fruit one is good, too, and less expensive to make.

1 cup sugar
4 cups water
8 inches vanilla bean, broken into 6 even
    lengths
1 large lime, halved lengthwise and sliced
    ⅛ inch thick
1 small orange, halved lengthwise and sliced
    about ¼ inch thick
3 packages (8 ounces each) dried apricots or 1
    package (8 ounces) each of dried apricots,
    dried peaches, and dried pears
6 tablespoons dark rum for apricots or the
    same amount of cognac-orange liqueur for
    mixed fruit

&#10070;Stir sugar and water together in a wide 2½-quart saucepan until no crystals remain. Tie vanilla bean in two thicknesses of dampened cheesecloth, or place in a small metal tea ball. Add the bean to the syrup, bring quickly to boil, lower heat, and boil 5 minutes. Add the lime and orange slices in a single layer, top with the dried fruit, and boil steadily over medium heat about 30 minutes. Stir the dried fruit occasionally without disturbing the citrus layer on the bottom. When the dried fruit is plump and tender, remove pan from heat, remove and reserve the vanilla bean, and stir in the rum or liqueur as soon as boiling stops.

Stir to mix the fruits well, and divide fruit and syrup among hot, sterilized jars. The syrup should be scant and thick, but make sure it covers the fruit, which will expand as it cools. Put 1 piece of vanilla bean on top in each half-pint jar or 2 pieces in pints. Seal at once, and invert jars until cool. Store at least a week for flavors to blend and peels to mellow and soften. Discard vanilla bean before serving. Makes about 6 cups.

# Vanilla Brandy

This flavoring is called for in several recipes in my book, and it also can be used instead of vanilla in baking and in puddings. A spoonful or two is delicious on fresh, frozen, or canned fruit, with or without syrup.

1 or 2 whole vanilla beans
1 pint brandy

🍓 Drop the beans into the bottle, reseal it, and let stand at least 2 weeks. It keeps indefinitely, and the beans can be reused until they lose their strength.

# Prunes in Port

A jar of this fruit keeps almost indefinitely at room temperature. The prunes are delicious plain, with a little of their port syrup, but they're even better served with sweet or sour cream and a dusting of sugar. Puréed, they add a whole new dimension to old-fashioned prune whip.

Quantities are hard to estimate. Some fruits absorb more liquid than others. I usually empty a 12-ounce package of pitted prunes into a clean, scalded apothecary jar with a plastic or ground glass stopper and cover the fruit by at least 1 inch with tawny port. After a couple of days, if the prunes expand above the surface of the port, I add more wine and reseal the jar. That's all. This usually takes 2 cups or more of port.

A mixture of prunes and apricots is also good, and for this I use:

12 ounces (1 box) pitted prunes
8 ounces (1 package) dried apricots
¼ cup sugar
3 cups tawny port

Put the ingredients in the order listed in a 1½-quart bowl, and cover tightly. When the fruit has plumped fully, and sugar has dissolved, pack into apothecary or canning jars and seal. The apricots will retain their chewiness and will darken after a few weeks almost as much as the prunes.

# Brandied Plums

In our American tradition, compotes are fruits stewed or cooked in syrup and usually served as dessert. I also like them, and this plum compote in particular, as an accompaniment to game and other roast meats. For dessert, the plums are good alone or with ice cream or unfrosted cakes, especially angel food. You might also use any leftover syrup on canned or frozen fruit or fresh fruit such as ripe peaches or pears.

2 pounds ripe Italian prune plums, each
    pierced 3 to 4 times with a small skewer
2 cups sugar
1 cup water
Cognac or vanilla brandy (page 188)

🍐Place prepared fruit in a deep 2-quart bowl. Bring sugar and water to boil in 1½-quart saucepan, stirring. Boil rapidly 5 minutes without stirring. Pour boiling syrup over plums, and stir to coat them. Weight with a saucer or plate and a jar of water. Let stand about 24 hours. The syrup will gradually cover the fruit.

The next day, sterilize 3 wide mouth pint jars and lids. Place plums and syrup in a wide 2½-quart saucepan over very low heat, and stir occasionally to heat the fruit evenly. When skins begin to tear in one or two places and plums are heated through, use a slotted spoon to place drained plums in the jars—about a dozen per jar—to fill three-quarters full. Boil the syrup rapidly about 10 minutes, to thicken slightly. Divide it among the jars, leaving approximately the top fourth of each one empty. Cover with a clean dish towel and let cool. Top off with the brandy of your choice, filling jars within about ¼ inch of the top, and seal. Invert for 24 hours, then turn right side up and store at least 3 months before using. I always set the jars in shallow trays to catch overflowing syrup during fermentation. When fermentation stops, remove the lids. Clean lids, jar threads, and rims and outside of the jars, then reseal.

# Brandied Pears

Anjou pears are best for this recipe, largely because of their compactness and uniform shape. The long, slim necks on Boscs and Bartletts tend to overcook before the thicker base is done. Comice pears usually are too large to pack easily, and they are so good fresh it seems a shame to cook them. Seckel and forelle pears could be used, but I find their firm texture more suitable for pickling than preserving. Pear brandy — *eau de vie de poire* — lends a truly splendid flavor to this dessert but makes it so expensive you may prefer to reserve pear brandy for drinking and use regular grape brandy instead.

> About 4¼ pounds or a dozen 5- to 6-ounce
>     firm, ripe (pale green) Anjou pears
> 2 teaspoons ascorbic acid mixture (page 201),
>     dissolved in 6 cups water
> 2 cups sugar
> 1½ cups water
> About 6 tablespoons eau de vie de poire or
>     other brandy per pint jar

♦ Peel, halve, and core the pears. Drop the pear halves, as you prepare them, into the ascorbic acid mixture and water in a bowl of at least 3-quart capacity. This helps prevent darkening. The easiest way to achieve uniform halves is to peel the whole fruit with a swivel-blade peeler, the kind you use for potatoes. Halve pears lengthwise, cut out stem and blossom ends with a small, sharp knife, and core with a small melon ball cutter.

Mix 1 cup of the sugar with the remaining 1½ cups of water in a wide 2½-quart saucepan. Bring quickly to boil, and boil rapidly 5 minutes. Add 6 pear halves, cut side up, and poach for about 5 minutes. Turn cut side down when they're half done. Continue poaching 5 to 10 minutes — until tender but still firm. Use a toothpick or small bamboo skewer for testing to avoid breaking the fruit. As each half is done, drain it well with a slotted spoon, and pack, cut side down, in hot, sterilized wide mouth jars, filling them within about ½ inch of the tops. You'll probably get 6 to 8 halves into each jar—the pears shrink and settle.

When all the pears are poached, drain excess syrup from jars back into the saucepan, add the remaining cup of sugar, and boil rapidly about 10 minutes, until syrup thickens slightly. Divide it among the jars, leaving room for the brandy, and let cool. When the jars are cool, add brandy and a small piece of wadded waxed paper to keep the fruit submerged in the syrup. Seal, and stand the jars in a shallow container to catch syrup that overflows during fermentation. When fermentation, or bubbling, stops, remove the lids, clean the threads, rims, and lids, and reseal. Store 2 or 3 months to mellow before using. The yield ranges between 4 and 5 pints, depending on the size of the pears. Fermentation time varies, depending on temperature, but it usually lasts several weeks.

*The Pleasures of Preserving and Pickling*

# Spiced Wine Vinegar

The inspiration for this salad vinegar was a recipe by Simone (Simca) Beck long before she became famous as an author and a colleague of Julia Child, public television's French Chef. I came across it in *What's Cooking in France,* a small book published in London in 1955. I have adapted Mme. Beck's recipe only to the extent of using ingredients readily available throughout the United States. My version is less acid than most vinegars and is particularly delicious in fruit salad dressings.

3 tablespoons anisette
3 tablespoons gin or 3 tablespoons vodka plus
   2 juniper berries, coarsely cracked
1 clove garlic, peeled and quartered
3 shallots, peeled and chopped, or half a small
   white onion and a clove of garlic, peeled
   and chopped
1 small yellow onion, peeled and studded
   with 5 cloves
6 whole anise seeds
3 whole black peppercorns, coarsely cracked
½ teaspoon dried leaf tarragon or 3 small
   sprigs fresh tarragon
4 cups wine vinegar

🍃 Place anisette, gin or vodka, and juniper berries, garlic, shallots, onion, anise, peppercorns, and tarragon in a wide mouth quart jar. Fill to within ¼ inch of top with vinegar, and reserve remaining vinegar for later use. Cover tightly, and let stand 3 weeks at room temperature. Then pour mixture through a strainer lined with two thicknesses of dampened cheesecloth. Stir in reserved vinegar, decant into sterilized bottles, and cover tightly. Makes about 4¼ cups.

# Pepper Wine or Pepper Sherry

These are piquant liquid seasonings from Barbados and Bermuda. Islanders use them as Americans do bottled red pepper sauces, shaking a few drops into soups, stews, and seafood. The method of preparation is the same on both islands, but Barbadians use white rum instead of wine, and the Bermudians use dry sherry. In the islands, fresh hot chili peppers would be called for, but the dried variety found in spice racks at supermarkets and specialty shops works equally well.

8 to 10 dried chilies, each about 1 inch long
1 pint white or light rum or dry sherry

❦ If you want to stabilize the peppers' strength, place the peppers in a clean, scalded 1½-pint Mason jar, add the rum or sherry, cover, and set in a dark cupboard for a week to 10 days. Shake the bottle occasionally. Then put the mixture through a strainer lined with a double layer of dampened cheesecloth, and funnel the clear liquid into a clean, narrow necked bottle with a screw lid. A vinegar bottle, the type that comes with both a removable plastic shaker cap and a regular cap, is ideal, or, for a gift, a pretty cruet with a shaker top.

Of course, you can simply put the chilies and the liquid in a jar and leave them, adding more rum or sherry as the liquid level drops, and discarding the chilies only when their strength diminishes.

## WARNING
Never taste pepper wine or pepper sherry alone—it is fiercely hot. Shake a drop or two onto a forkful of fish or meat or into a tablespoon of soup instead. If it's too strong, just add more rum or sherry to reduce the potency.

# Lemon- or Orange-Flavored Mustard

Both of these mustards are delicious with hot or cold fish or seafood, pork, ham, cold roast duck, even cold roast beef. Like all prepared mustards, the peppery flavor grows milder once the jars have been opened, so if you plan to use these condiments as gifts, make them as late as possible and be sure to tell the recipients to refrigerate them to conserve the mustards' strength as long as possible.

1 jar (8 ounces) Dijon-style prepared mustard
½ teaspoon lemon or orange extract
2 teaspoons freshly grated lemon or orange
   peel, the colored part only (from 1 lemon or
   ½ orange)

Use a rubber scraper to remove as much mustard as possible from its jar into a bowl of at least 1½-cup capacity. Stir in the extract and peel, blend well, and return mixture to original jar, or, for gift giving, a small apothecary jar with a tight stopper. Refrigerate. Makes about 1 cup.

# Glossary

**Airtight seal:** See *Seal, vacuum.*

**Alum:** A fine white powder, ammonium alum, sold at drugstores and, in pickling seasons, at grocery spice racks. In pickling, it is used in minute amounts to help keep vegetables and fruits crisp.

**Ascorbic acid:** Vitamin C, which is widely available in drugstores and health food stores in tablet form. In preserving and pickling it helps prevent browning of fruits such as peaches and pears.

**Ascorbic acid mixture:** A blend of sugar, ascorbic acid powder, and an anticaking agent that serves the same purpose as plain ascorbic acid. It is sold in food stores in areas where much canning and preserving is done and sometimes can be found in drugstores as well.

**Blanch:** To cover with, and sometimes cook briefly in, boiling water. Some fruits are blanched so they can be peeled easily. Walnuts need blanching to prevent browning of other ingredients in conserves and compotes.

**Boil, full rolling:** Large bubbles rise and break on surface of a liquid so rapidly that vigorous stirring does not interfere.

**Boil, steady:** Medium to large bubbles rise regularly to surface of a liquid and break there, but reduced bubbling occurs when liquid is stirred.

**Butter, fruit:** Fruit purée cooked with sugar to a consistency that spreads like butter. Butters usually are spicy.

**Calcium hydroxide U.S.P.:** A white powder, formerly called slaked lime, that is used in preserving and pickling to help keep acid fruits and vegetables crisp. It is also used in pharmaceuticals, petrochemicals, cements, mortar, and farming and gardening. Only the pure pharmaceutical type should be used for canning.

**Canning, open kettle:** Preserving foods by cooking them in uncovered saucepans and packing them, usually while hot, in hot, sterilized jars, which are then sealed, cooled, and stored.

**Canning, pressure:** Processing sealed jars of food under pressure at 240 degrees Fahrenheit (at sea level to 2,000 feet above; adjustments must be made at higher altitudes). This method is necessary for low-acid foods to destroy bacteria which can cause spoilage and food poisoning, including botulism. See page 31 for additional information.

**Canning, water bath:** Processing certain acid and/or sweet foods to destroy bacteria, enzymes, molds, and yeasts that can cause spoilage. Filled, sealed jars are boiled (or simmered) for specific lengths of time in water deep enough to cover them by an inch or so at top and bottom. For additional information, see page 30.

**Chutney:** A pungent relish of East Indian origin made from fruit, herbs, and spices.

**Compote:** Fruit cooked or stewed in syrup.

**Conserve:** Crushed or ground fruit made from a mixture that usually contains some citrus and often raisins and nuts as well.

**Funnel, canning:** A wide-stemmed funnel designed to fit the necks of standard home canning (Mason) jars.

**Head space:** Air space between the top of the food and the jar lid. It allows for expansion during cooling and/or freezing.

**Jam:** A mixture of crushed and/or ground fruit that tends to hold its shape but usually is not as firm as jelly.

**Jars, Mason:** Glass containers with threaded necks made especially for home canning, pickling, and preserving. They range in size from half-pint (1 cup) to half-gallon. Most brands use two-part self-sealing lids. Tapered Mason jars, larger at the mouth than at the base, can be used for freezing as well as canning.

**Jell test:** See page 42.

**Jelly:** A clear spread made from fruit juice (or wine and pectin) that is firm enough to hold its shape when turned out of its container.

**Lid, self-sealing:** A two-part metal closure consisting of an enamel-lined metal lid with sealing compound and a threaded metal band, or ring, to hold the lid in place. When used as a manufacturer directs, it produces a vacuum seal that can be verified by the position of the lid after a jar's contents have cooled. Directions for use come with packages of lids, bands and lids, and cases of jars. All are packed in units of twelve.

**Marmalade:** Tender jelly with fruit suspended evenly in it. Most contain citrus fruit.

**Preserves:** Whole fruits or large pieces in a thick syrup that may be slightly jellied.

**Salt, pickling or canning:** Medium crystal salt packed without additives that interfere with the pickling process. Sold in 5-pound bags and 26-ounce round cardboard containers.

**Salt, coarse (kosher):** Large crystal salt processed with only a tiny amount of anticaking agent and no additives that interfere with pickling. If pickling or canning salt is unavailable, coarse (kosher) salt is preferable to table salt for most recipes using cucumbers.

**Scald:** Rinse with boiling water.

**Seal, vacuum:** Airtight seal that helps preserve food. In general, it can be recognized with home canning jars and lids when the center of a self-sealing lid is depressed and remains that way after a jar has cooled. Occasionally, it is necessary to tap the center lightly with a finger to complete a seal. If the lid pops up again, the jar should be either repacked, following the original directions, or used promptly. If the food does not require prolonged storage for mellowing (as most pickles and relishes do), check the recipe to see if the unsealed jar should be refrigerated or stored at room temperature.

**Simmer:** Tiny bubbles rise slowly and break below surface of a cooking liquid, so that it barely shivers.

# Source List

All of the ingredients and utensils called for in this book are sold at retail stores, but specific items may not always be available in every community. However, manufacturers usually will provide the name of the nearest retail dealer on request; and some manufacturers sell certain items by mail direct to consumers. The following list is intended as a guide.

**Ascorbic acid mixture** (food stores and drugstores): Fruit-Fresh Brand, Consumer Division, Calgon Corp., Box 1346, Pittsburgh, Pa. 15230.

**Calcium hydroxide U.S.P., formerly slaked lime** (drugstores): Public Relations Department, Eli Lilly Co., Corporate Center, 307 East McCarty, Indianapolis, Ind. 46206.

**A product labeled Mrs. Wages Pickling Lime:** Sold in some Southern and Midwestern groceries during pickling seasons. It is packed by Dacus, Inc., Tupelo, Miss. 38801. Directions for use are on package.

**Herbs and spices, spice oils, fresh and crystallized ginger, vanilla beans:** Aphrodisia, 28 Carmine St., New York, N.Y. 10014 (catalog, $1). Some druggists also carry spice oils in their prescription departments.

**Herbs and spices, parchment paper, utensils, rock candy, and dried fruit:** H. Roth and Son, 1577 First Ave., New York, N.Y. 10028 (catalog); The Spice Box, 968 Second Ave., New York, N.Y. 10022; Paprikas Weiss, 1546 Second Ave., New York, N.Y. 10028 (catalog).

**Jars, lids, and utensils, including jar lifters and/or squeeze tongs** (housewares, hardware, variety, and some department stores and food chains): Retailers in New York include: Bridge Co., 212 East 52 St., New York, N.Y. 10022; Bazaar de la Cuisine, 1003 Second Ave., New York, N.Y. 10022. Jar lifters can also be ordered by mail from: Consumer Products Division, Kerr Glass Manufacturing Co., Sand Springs, Okla. 74063. Jar lifters and other canning accessories made by Leisure Technology, Inc., 1615 West River Road North, Minneapolis, Minn., 55416 are sold in retail stores in all fifty states. For address of store nearest you, write manufacturer. For information about availability of squeeze tongs, write: Kenneth Fischer, Sales Manager, Acme Metal Goods Mfg. Co., 2 Orange St., Newark, N.J. 17102.

**Shallots, fresh:** Food stores or by mail from George N. Levari, 51 DeShibe Terrace, Vineland, N.J. 08360.

**Thermometer, spoon type** (housewares, hardware, variety, and department stores): Manufacturer: Gaydell, Inc., 3030 Wilshire Blvd., Santa Monica, Ca. 90403.

# General Index

*(Recipe index follows on page 205)*

# Recipe Index

# A NOTE ABOUT THE AUTHOR

Jeanne Lesem was born in Leavenworth, Kansas, and grew up in small towns in Arkansas during the Depression. She learned to cook while helping her mother prepare meals in the family's large, old-fashioned kitchen in North Little Rock, Arkansas. In 1956, Ms. Lesem originated the weekly cooking column for United Press, now United Press International. Currently food and family living editor for the news agency, she does most of her cooking these days under less-than-ideal conditions — in an 8- by 9-foot Manhattan apartment kitchen with a single-oven four burner gas range and a minimum of counter and storage space. Like many other home-taught cooks, Ms. Lesem tends to tamper with recipes and believes that every cook should be encouraged to improvise. This is her first book.

# A NOTE ABOUT THE TYPE

The text of this book was set in film in Melior, a typeface designed by Hermann Zapf and issued in 1952. Born in Nürnberg, Germany, in 1918, Zapf has been a strong influence in printing since 1939. Melior, like Times Roman, another popular twentieth-century typeface, was created specifically for use in a newspaper. With this functional end in mind, Zapf nonetheless chose to base the proportions of its letterforms on those of the Golden Section. The result is a typeface of unusual strength and surpassing subtlety.

Composed by American Can Company, Printing Division, Clarinda, Iowa. Printed and bound by The Book Press, Brattleboro, Vermont. Typography and binding design by Christine Aulicino.